# The Yoga Sutras:
# The Path to Inner Liberation and Harmony

*Swami Divyananda*

GRAPEVINE INDIA

Published by

**GRAPEVINE INDIA PUBLISHERS PVT LTD**

www.grapevineindia.com

Delhi | Mumbai

email: grapevineindiapublishers@gmail.com

Ordering Information:

Quantity sales: Special discounts are available on quantity purchases by corporations, associations, and others.

For details, reach out to the publisher.

First published by Grapevine India 2024

# Introduction

The Yoga Sūtras of Patañjali are a collection of 196 Sanskrit sutras on the theory and practice of yoga. The Yoga Sutras were compiled sometime between 500 BCE and 400 CE by the sage Patanjali in India who synthesized and organized knowledge about yoga from much older traditions. Patañjali was a sage in India, thought to be the author of a number of Sanskrit works. The greatest of these are the Yoga Sutras, one of the most important texts in the Indian tradition and the foundation of classical Yoga. It is the Indian Yoga text that was most translated in its medieval era into forty Indian languages.

Sutras (in Sanskrit) literally means a thread or string that holds things together and more metaphorically refers to an aphorism. The Yoga Sutras by Patanjali is an ancient philosophy that enlightens one in the knowledge of yoga, its origin, and the ultimate purpose. Its purpose is to make the principles and practices of the Yoga formulae more understandable and accessible for all. In the Yoga Sutras, practical and easy suggestions are presented through which one can experience the ultimate benefits of a yogic lifestyle. The Yoga Sutras of Patanjali are life's threads, each one rich with knowledge, tools, and techniques. These sutras guide not only the mind but also one's very being to its full potential. Patanjali's Yoga Sutras offer a systematic form of wisdom for attaining self-realization/enlightenment.

# What are Yoga Sutras?

If you're new to the world of yoga, you might not have encountered the ancient wisdom encapsulated in the Yoga Sutras of Patanjali. In essence, these sutras consist of 196 concise verses that serve as a roadmap to attain wisdom and self-realization through the practice of yoga. These teachings are believed to have been composed around 400 C.E. and are highly regarded as the foundational principles of yoga philosophy.

The 196 sutras, which can be translated as "threads" or "discourses," are categorized into four chapters or padas: Samadhi, Sadhana, Vibhuti, and Kaivalya. While the text is open to various interpretations, its core purpose is to provide profound and practical wisdom to guide practitioners, both novices and experienced yogis and yoginis, on their journey to understand the essence of yoga.

# Samadhi Padas

The initial chapter of the Yoga Sutras of Patanjali delves into the essence of yoga itself. This section comprises 51 sutras that resonate with those who have already integrated yoga into their daily lives. It explores themes such as enlightenment, concentration, and meditation.

# Sadhana Padas

Continuing through the book, the second chapter offers insights into how one can attain a yogic state. This section encompasses 55 sutras that discuss the practice of yoga and introduce the eight limbs of yoga, which encompass principles of ethics, conduct, and various facets of the yoga practice.

# Vibhuti Padas

Chapter three, consisting of 56 sutras, delves into the myriad benefits of consistent yoga practice. Here, Patanjali explores the transformative power of yoga and delves deeper into the final two limbs of yoga – Dhyana and Samadhi.

# Kaivalya Padas

The final chapter, comprising 34 sutras, focuses on liberation and the freedom from suffering. In this section, the text explores the ultimate goals of yoga and provides profound insights into the unconditional and absolute liberation that yoga offers.

Whether you're taking your first steps into yoga or you've been practicing for decades, the Yoga Sutras of Patanjali always offer something new to discover and learn.

# 1
# Samādhi pāda
# (Meditative Absorption)

The first chapter is about the deepest forms of meditation which are called *samadhi*.

# Verse 1

atha yoganusasanam

atha-now; yoganusasana = yoga- yoga and its practice = anusasanam-explanation

*Now I give the explanation of (the discipline of) yoga and its practice. Discipline is the basis of meditation and yoga. The word "Anushasan" also means discipline and regularity absolutely necessary for success in any human endeavour.*

## Commentary:

Sri Patanjali began by the term atha which means now or at this time, I will do something. He took the task of giving the explanation of yoga and its practice, because before this time such an explanation was not laid out in an academic way. He gave the syllabus for yoga, thus breaking the monopoly of all those teachers who mastered yoga and who taught it to their students bit by bit over the years.

Whatever Sri Patanjali would say would be standard. It cannot be changed merely by a difference in philosophy. Just as a gasoline combustion engine manufactured in Japan will be quite similar to one manufactured in German, so yoga practice will be the same everywhere, because the human body is the same in each case, and the way of changing the subtle form which produced that gross one is also the same.

# Verse 2

**yogah cittavrtti nirodhah**

**yogah- the skill of yoga; cittavritti = citta mento-emotional energy +vritti-vibrational mode; nirodhah - cessation, restraint, non operation**

*The skill of yoga is demonstrated by the conscious non-operation of the vibrational modes of the mento-emotional energy.*

## Commentary:

Yoga is something personal and practical. It is not a group effort. Each student of yoga has to achieve the states all by himself or herself. Thus in a sense, yoga is an isolated and lonely course. This is the reason for the poor response of the public to the call to take up hard-core yoga austerities. People like company but yoga requires the company of one's self only. One must work with one's psyche only to be successful in yoga.

There were many attempts to translate the word *citta.* Some say it is the mind, some say it is the energy in the mind. Some say it is the consciousness. These terms, though accurate to a degree bring with them a certain vagueness which covers the meaning even more.

To understand *citta* we have to consider two aspects, those of thinking and feeling. Whatever energy is used for thinking is citta, and whatever is used for feeling is citta. It is citta through which we think and feel. To understand citta one has to become concerned with psychological locations. Where does your thinking take place? When a thought arises in which energy is illustrated in the mind? When you have an emotional response to something real or imaginary, in which part of your psyche does that take place? What sort of energy is used to develop and transmit emotion? Whatever correct answer one would give to any of these questions would identify the citta energy. Chitta is the mento-emotional energy in which our thoughts are formed and are disintegrated. It is the energy in which our feelings are formed and in which the same feelings subside to nothingness.

By convention it is discovered that the vibrational energy of the mind always keeps moving in one way or the other. Thus some spiritual masters conclude that it would be impossible to comply with this stipulation of Patanjali for the non-operation of the mento-emotional force in the psyche. They have dismissed Patanjali as being an impractical theorist. The solution they say is to engage the mind in spiritual topics, never giving it the chance to dwell on ordinary subjects which are apart from the trancendence. However, human convention is not everything. When a yogin gets experience beyond the dimension of this world, he can afford to heed Patanjali, and strive for the non-operation of the mental-emotional force in this dimension of consciousness. Somehow by his own endeavor and by divine grace, a yogin's mento-emotional force becomes stilled. It stalls for a time and turns into a divine vision which perceives the *chit akasha*, the sky of consciousness. The world known otherwise as akshardam, brahma and vaikuntha. When this happens , the yogi understands what Sri Patanjali explained in this verse 2 of his sutras.

Srila Yogeshwaranana Yogiraja indicated that Sri Patanjali should not have suggested that it was possible to completely quiet the mento-emotional force, for indeed, it is not possible to stop it from vibrating altogether, but rather one may quiet it in one dimension while it continues to operate in another. It cannot be quieted in all of it's phases because even after the dissolution of the universe, the prana, or subtle mundane energy keeps shifting quietly for many millions of years. This slight movement, might in reference , be considered to be static but does have a vibrational consistency.

# Verse 3

tada drastuh svarupe avasthanam

**tada- then; drastuh- the perceiver; svarupe- in his own form; avasthanam- is situated**

*Then the perceiver is situated in his own form.*

## Commentary:

When the mento-emotional energy has reached the state of quiescence, the perceiver within that energy, experiences himself by himself, alone without those influences. This is the state of swarupa, or his own form.

So long as that mento-emotional energy vibrates actively, the perceiver is not allowed to reflect on himself. He is instead, drawn into concerns other than myself. Thus he responds carelessly since his sense of identity was diverted to something else.. Sri Patanjali gave this statement about the situation in the spiritual self, swarupe, to give encouragement and to generate interest in self realization. After all, if one does not realize one's essential self, one must identify with objects or energies which are not the self.

# Verse 4

## vrtti sarupyam itaratra

**vritti-** the mento-emotional energy; **sarupayam-** with the same format, conformity; **itaratra -** at other times

*At other times, there is conformity with the mento-emotional energy.*

### Commentary:

The perceiver, even though he is different to the mento-emotional energy, is not allowed to show autonomy or independence when that energy is active in its concern for things in this dimension. The perceiver is forced as it were, to conform to the dictates of that mento-emotional force. He is forced to use the same format as the energy irrespective of a deliberate or non-deliberate interest into this dimension and its corresponding higher or lower locales. The perceiver is forced to identify with that ideation energy. It is only when its vibrations cease of their own accord or are suppressed by him or by another force, that he may realize the self.

# Verse 5

**vrttayah pancatayyah klista aklistah**

**vrttayah-** the vibrations in mento-emotional energy; **pancatayyah -** fivefold; **klistaklistah= klista-** agonizing + **aklistah-** non-troublesome

*The vibrations in the mento-emotional energy are five-fold being agonizing or none- troublesome.*

**Commentary:**

Sri Patanjali has not given a middle designation or a mixed status for the mento-emotional vibrations. He simply stated that there were five types of these vibrations; some causing agony and some which are not troublesome. This is to be realized in mystic yoga practice so that the yogi becomes expert at recognizing the various moods of his mind and emotions. An ignorance of the operations of the mental and emotional energy, will cause the self to trail behind the mental and emotional moods. This will invariably lead to haphazard rebirths and responsibility for wreckless acts. Ignorance of one's psychology and of how it operates, is costly to the living entity.

As stated in the second verse of these sutras, the skill of yoga is demonstrated by non-vibrational of the mento-emotional energies. When the Yogi ceases the vibrations, the energy converts into being a supernatural vision with which he sees into the chit-akash, the sky of consciousness, the spiritual environment. The yogin was given the citta energy for that purpose but due to his ineptness he was not able to use it appropriately. Instead it served him for imagining and analyzing mundane energy. Sri Patanjali will tell us something more about the five vibrationial modes of the mental and emotional energy.

# Verse 6

pramana viparyaya vikalpa nidra smrtayah

pramana - correct perception; viparyaya - incorrect perception; vikalpa – imagination; nidra – sleep; smrtayah- memory

*They are correct perception, incorrect perception, imagination, sleep and memory.*

## Commentary:

This means that we have to recognize five kinds of vibrational activities of the mento-emotional energy. According to Sri Patanjali whatever occurs in the mental and emotional energy must be one of a combination of the five vibrations. A yogin should know these thoroughly. If one does not understand the workings of his mind and feelings, he cannot become liberated. One cannot become liberated from an ignorance of these.

We are endowed with the mento-emotional energy and it is restricted to those five kinds of vibrations which produce either correct perception , false perception, imagination, sleep and memory. All these psychological functions occur in the citta energy. That is its capability when focused into this dimension. The problem with this is that the living entity cannot always be in a position to know what is taking place within his own mind and emotions. In most persons, the operations occur faster than the entity is able to perceive. Thus the entity sees the conclusions or feels such conclusion and does not understand what is taking place until after it has occurred or until after he or she has reacted beneficially or unbeneficially to them.

Let us take for example the operation of sleep. One may fall asleep and not know it until after the sleep mode has terminated. A man for instance, who drives a car in a tired state, would realize that he fell asleep at the wheel after his car had crashed into a tree and he awoke in a badly damaged body in a hospital. The operations are impulsively performed in the mind and emotions. This impulsiveness is a handicap for the living entity.

Now will discuss these five operations one by one.

*Correct Perception:*

The most interesting feature of this operation is our dependence upon it. The question arises as to why we need a psychological tool for correct perception. Why is it that we could not perceive reality without having to use the mento-emotional energy? The question is this: If as this sutra indicates , we are dependent on the correct perception vibrational mode of the mind, then how can we restrict the energy so that it does not shift into the mode which gives us incorrect perception or unrealistic imagination? As we consider these sutras, we will see if Sri Patanjali dealt with these questions. Otherwise each yogi will have to get answers from another authority and from his own valid research.

The only thing we know for certain is this: the mento-emotional energy is capable of five kinds of operations. Furthermore, normally we do not control this, but rather this happens reflexively. What yoga process gives us the ability to control this either absolutely or partially?

*Incorrect perception:*

The problem with false perception is that within the energy itself, there is a tendency not to recognize the vibrations which cause false perception, but rather to try to correct such perception by various haphazard applications. Therefore we have to train the psychology in a different way, in a totally new way, so that it becomes concerned only with recognizing the vibrational state from which false perceptions are derived. This means that we have to advance to higher yoga in dharana linkage of the mind to higher concentration forces.

It is not false perceptions that are the problem but rather the vibrations in the energy which cause the wrong views in the first place. We have to strive to recognize these vibrations and to stop them, so that the mind may function only with the vibrations which produce correct or true perceptions. This will take repeated practice, because the vibrations which produce false perceptions are naturally occurring. It is not a matter of suppressing these undesirable vibrations, even though a yogi will have to suppress them from time to time. It is rather a feat for the yogi to cause the mind and feelings not to vibrate in that way. This would require a mastership of pranayama and a strong development of vigilance and acute dispassion. These aspects will be discussed in detail elsewhere in this commentary. It is mentioned by Sri Patanjali.

# Verse 7

## pratyaksa anumana agamah pramanani

**pratyaksanumanagamah= pratyaksa- direct but correct perception + anumana- correct analysis + agamah- correct reference; pramanani- true perception, correct perception**

*Correct perception may be acquired directly, by correct analysis or by correct reference.*

### Commentary:

Even though this is obvious, Sri Patanjali alerts us in this verse, that we have to learn how to recognize when our intellect functions in this mode of operation. Everyone understands that when false information is used there will be incorrect conclusions. Analysis, when applied to false information, results in false conclusion, which leads to incorrect insight. It is the same with reference. A reference may be the wrong one, or it may be inaccurate, hence the use of it will lead to false conclusions. Direct perception may be incorrect. Pratyaksa is a combination of prati and akshah, but aksha means perception. When that perception is correct, it is prati-aksha, pratyaksa. For true perception a yogin must have an accurate intellect and also have accurate information from outside his intellect. It is not just reliant on his intellect. It is reliant on getting accurate information outside the intellect. However, if the yogin's intellect is sufficiently surcharged with higher concentration forces, he will recognize the incorrect and unreliable information. He will not use such information to produce wrong conclusions. A yogi must be in the right position to get the right information. This is achieved by mystic maneuvers. This all means that there is more for accurate perception; more is required besides the purity of the psyche of the yogi. He has to get himself into a position from which he can use his accurate buddhi organ to perceive correctly.

An astronomer may have an accurate telescope but still he cannot take an accurate reading on a very cloudy night unless he can go beyond the cloud formations. He has to put himself in the proper positions to use the accurate instrument. Correct perception may be acquired directly only if the yogin has a reality-perceiving intellect and is in the proper position to use it.

Correct perception can be acquired directly by insight developed by correct analysis after getting some facts but this is solidified only after the yogin can take that analysis to the point of getting the direct sight of it. Furthermore, by correct reference, a yogin may form certain correct conclusions but that is not sufficient because it is not direct sensual observation. Therefore it is incomplete. He will have to develop himself further to reach the stage of true direct sensual perception of the supernatural and spiritual realities.

Finally a yogin has to develop himself in such a way as to sort out the various true and erroneous perceptions of his intellect. Then he may suppress and gradually eliminate the faulty parts and the motivations which support defective perception.

# Verse 8

**viparyayah mithyajnanam atadrupa pratistham**

viparyaah - incorrect perception; mithyajnanam= mithya-false + jnanam-information; atadrupa = atad - not this = rupa- form; pratistham - positioned, based

*Incorrect perception is based on false information and on perception of what is not the true form.*

## Commentary:

The vibrational mode which produces a firm conviction about something that is incorrect is caused by the perception of false information and on perceiving what is not the true form (atadrupa).

The willingness of the buddhi organ in accepting the information given to it by the senses is the root of this problem. The reliance of the buddhi on the sensual energies must be broken by the yogin. This can be achieved by perfecting the pratyahar 5th stage of yoga practice, where the sensual energies are withdrawn from their interest into the subtle and gross mundane world. The strength of the senses which is their ability to keep the buddhi organ under subjugation is based on the extrovert tendencies of the organ. Thus if that tendency is squelched, the senses lose their authority over the organ and it becomes independent of them. This is mastered by pratyahar practice.

The perception of the sensual energies is operated with the energy of fuel of the prana which is subtle air. When the yogi practices pranayama and is able to take in a higher grade of prana, his senses become purified and they no longer make so many erroneous judgments which they force the buddhi to accept. Thus the yogi becomes freed from incorrect perceptions.

# Verse 9

sabdajnana anupati vastusunyah vikalpah

**sabdajnana** – written or spoken information; **anupati-** followed by; **vastusunyah-** devoid of reality, without reality; **vikalpah-** imagination

*Verbal or written information which is followed by concepts which are devoid of reality, is imagination.*

## Commentary:

It is important to understand that the same mento-emotional energy which can mislead the living entity or cause him to come to the wrong conclusion, is the very same psychic organ which he must use to see into the super-physical world. Even though Sri Patanjali listed only five modes of operation for this tool, still, when it is shifted off from this world it can be used for super-physical perceptions. Therefore it can be used in the mode of correct perceptions for spiritual insights.

When it is used as motivated by false verbal or written information, it develops ideas, conceptions and the like, which cause an imagination which has no basis in reality. But since the living entity is dependent on it, he accepts its picturizations, sounds and impressions as if such notions were a reality. Thus he makes mistakes. He has to learn to recognize when his buddhi organ has adopted a submissive acceptance of incorrect information.

# Verse 10

abhava pratyaya alambana vrttih nidra

abhava- absence of awareness; pratyaya- conviction or belief as mental content; alambana- support, prop, means of conversion; vrittih- vibrational mode; nidra - sleep

*Sleep is the vibrationial mode which is supported by the absence of objective awareness.*

### Commentary:

There are various types of sleep but the true sleep is when the mind has no content, such that one feels as if one was barely existing during the sleep. This is realized not during that state but after it. During such sleep the living entity becomes disconnect from his buddhi organ. But when he is connected to it again, he realizes that he was barely connect to his discrimination and sense of objectivity.

We may consider that the vritties or vibrational modes of the mental and emotional energy are fivefold in normal consciousness. It is like a car which has a set of four gears, with a mental functioning. The reverse function is comparable to the operational mode of memory. Memory has to do with recalling something from the past. The mental function is comparable to deep sleep when the vehicle cannot move at all. The other modes or gears are all forward vibrations, which Sri Patanjali gave as correct perception, false perception and imagination.

# Verse 11

anubhuta visaya asampramosah smrtih

**anubhuta- the experience; visaya- the object; asampramosah- retention; smrtih- memory**

*Memory is the retained impression of experienced objects.*

## Commentary:

Memory has to do with the past and therefore it might be compared to the reverse gear in an automobile. In reverse, the driver travels on the path traversed before. Memory must be curbed by a yogin, because otherwise he would never be free from the mental impressions which have formed in his conscious and subconscious mind. These impressions vent themselves into the conscious mind and are appropriated by the buddhi intellect organ for usages in further imaginations, which lead to actions of interference in the material world. This interference brings on liabilities for which the yogin is held responsible. If one does not quell, or quiet off completely, the memory and disconnect from the memory, he cannot become liberated. Thus a yogin has to get a method of removing this function in the mento-emotional energy.

# Verse 12

## abhyasa vairagyabhyam tannirodhah

abhysa- effective yoga practice; vairagyabhyam = non – interest, a total lack of concern, non- interference; tan= tat- that; nirodhah- cessation, restraint, non-operation

*That non-operation of the vibrational modes is achieved by effective practice in not having an interest n the very same operations.*

### Commentary:

Sri Patanjali Mahamuni Yogiraja gave me a hint regarding this verse. By telepathy he sent this clarification. "Those who are advanced should continue practicing with firm faith that their connection with the lower operational modes of the mental and emotional energies decreases daily. They need not read any more of these sutras which I wrote down so long ago.

"However those who are not so advanced should read further and take hints according to their particular progressions. In this verse twelve, these sutras are concluded, but dull students need to hear more from the teacher. They should listen to more of the verses. This book ends in this verse twelve for those who are advanced, but others should read on for more hints on practice."

To wipe out one's connection with the vrittis or the operational modes of the mental and emotional energies, we need to be detached from the very same operations or modes. That is all we need to do. However for those of use who are not so advanced we need to hear more. Basically speaking we have to enter into the neutral mode and from there into higher concentration energies which cause sensual perception into the chitakash, the sky of consciousness.

Vairagya has come to be translated as detachment or non attachment. However it is more than that . It is a total lack of interest and an attitude of non-interference in cultural activities. One gets hints about this as one progresses in yoga. One is shown the way by other great yogins like Sri Patanjali.

# Verse 13

**tatra sthitau yatnah abhyasah**

tatra – there, in that case; sthitau – regarding steadiness or persistence; yatnah - endeavor; abhyasah – practice

*In that case, practice is the persistent endeavor (to cultivate that lack of interest).*

## Commentary:

The related practice is hereby defined. It must be persistent and requires endeavor (yatnah). One has to cultivate that lack of interest because by nature, the mind and emotions are extroverted and have self-conceited mentality. The self-conceited mentality is used to enjoy privately in the psychology in a perverted and harmful way. All this must be curbed effectively.

# Verse 14

sa tu dirghakala nairantarya satkara asevitah drdhabhumih

sa =sah- that; tu- but; dirgha – long; kala- time; nairantarya-uninterrupted continuous; satkara—revernce, care attention; asevitah-sustained practice, aggressive interest; drdha- firm; bhumih- ground, foundation, basis

*But that is attained on the firm basis of a continuous reverential sustained practice which is executed for a long time.*

## Commentary:

What was acquired over millions and millions of births will take some time for its removal from the psyche.  It will not go away over night. Thus this yoga course is not the same as the easy paths of salvation.

# Verse 15

drsta anusravika visaya vitrsnasya vasikarasamjna vairagyam

drsta- what is seen or perceived directly; anusravika- what is conjectured on the basis of scripture or valid testimony; visya- an attractive object; vitrsnasya - of one who does not crave; vasikara – through control; samjna – consciousness, demeanor, mind-set; vairagyam- non interest

*The non interest in the operations of the mento-emotional energy is achieved by one who has perfect mastery in consciousness and who does not crave for what is perceived or what is heard of in the mundane existence.*

## Commentary:

To silence the mento-emotional energy one has to stop craving the subtle and gross existence. Any craving triggers a renewed interest in this world and its activities, that activates the five vibrational operations, which were listed before as correct perception, incorrect perception, imagination, memory and sleep.

# Verse 16

tatparam purusakhyateh gunavaitrsnyam

tat – that; param – highest (non – interest ); purusa - of the spiritual person; khyateh –of a thorough awareness; guna – features of material nature; vaitrsnyam – freedom from desire

*That highest non-interest occurs when there is freedom from desire for the features of material nature and thorough awareness of the spiritual person.*

## Commentary:

This does not come about easily. This is why Sri Patanjali alerted the student yogis that it will take a long time (dirgha kala) for them to attain success. This cultivation of non-interest is said to be part of raja yoga, but that does not mean that one can get it by avoiding asana and pranayama practice.

Purusha, the spirual personality and prakriti, the gross and subtle material nature, display a liking for one another. It is not an easy task for anyone to nullify this affinity. A complete transformation in the psychology would be required for one to develop the full non-interest in the subtle or gross mundane energy.

# Verse 17

**vitarka vicara ananda asmitarupa anugamat samprajnatah**

**vitarka** – analysis; **vicara** deliberation, reflection; **ananda** – introspective happiness; **asmitarupa** – I- ness self consciousness; **anugamat** - by accompaniment, occurring with; **samprajnatah** - the observational linkage of the attention to a higher concentration force

*The observational linkage of the attention to a higher concentration force occurs with analysis, reflection, introspective happiness or focus on self consciousness.*

## Commentary:

Suddenly and without warning, Sri Patanjali jumped from the cultivation of non-interest in the mundane world to the observational linkage of the attention to higher concentration force. If a yogin is successful at stopping the ordinary functions of his mento-emotional energies, he will enter a neutral stage from which his attention will be linked to or fused to higher concentration forces in the sky of consciousness , the chit akasha.

In the beginning the yogi will be affected by four other forces from this side of existence. These are the analytical power of the intellect, the reflective mood of it, the introspective happiness which is felt during pratyahar sensual withdrawal practice and the I-ness or self consciousness which has directed the attention to be linked to the higher concentration force.

Some other commentators categorized samprajnata as a type of samadhi. In other words it has come down in the yogic disciplic succession that samprajnatah is a type of samadi or a lower stage of the eighth and final level of yoga practice. However, this writer wants to inform readers that samprajnata is part of dharana practice which is the sixth stage of yoga. In that stage the linkage is deliberate and is done by the yogi by the mystic force applied . In the next stage, that of dhyana, the yogi is able to realize his sense of identity and his forceful application. He finds that his will power is drawn into the higher concentration force of it's own accord. In the eighth stage, that of samadhi, his will is not only effortlessly drawn but it is continually pulled like that for a long time, for over half hour or so.

In the stage of samdhi, he loses himself more and more, because he does not have to exert his will or deliberation. Thus he becomes relaxed. His mystic power loses tension and application because it is effortlessly pulled into and fused to the higher concentration force.

In the samprajnata observational linkage, the yogin sometimes finds that he must analyze what he is linked to. This is preliminary. All yogis go through these stages one by one as they progress and one does not move from lower to a higher stage until one has integrated the lower progression. At first when the deliberate linkage occurs, there is an analysis of what one is linked to, as to what level it is on and as to its value, as to what it will evolve into and as to the extent of transcendence.

After this one reflects on it, for the purpose of integrating it fully for the sake of being able to explain it to others at a later date. Many of the writings of this writer were made on the basis of due reflection in this stage. It is for the integration of the writer himself and use later on in teaching and explaining. After one advanced beyond this, one reaches a stage of introspective happiness. This is due to full pratyahar when one loses interest in others and totally pulls in all sensual energies and is able to direct oneself purely without looking back for others.

When this stage is completed, one reaches a stage of self awareness in feeling the limits of one's spiritual radiation. At this stage one links up with the cosmic buddhi and the cosmic sense of identity which are bright lights on the super physical planes of existence. This causes an enrichment of one's personality and a surcharging of one's spirituality. If one is not careful at this stage, one may attract many disciples, thus bring one's spiritual practice to an end.

# Verse 18

viramapratyaya abhyasapurvah samskarasesah anyah

virama – losing track of, dropping; prayaya – objective awareness, opinions and motives of mind content; abhyasa – practice; purvah-previous, before; samskarasesah + samskara – impression in the mento-emotional energy =sesah – what is remaining; anyah – other

*The other state is the compete departure from the level where the remaining impressions lie in the mento-emotional energy.*

## Commentary:

The previous practice of losing track of one's opinions and motives results in the other state which is awareness of remaining impressions left in the mento-emotional energy.

Most commentators agree that this is the stage of asamprajnata samadhi or a state of fusion to a higher plane without maintaining any opinions or motivations.

Provided that one has had a previous practice of repeatedly losing track of one's opinions and motivations, one can attain this other state in which there is awareness of the remaining impressions in their seed form as they exist in the mind compartment and in the emotions. The yogi must repeatedly practice to attain this, as Sri Patanjali told us of the long practice (dirgha kala) required. In this state there is no foothold on any form or forms, and therefore the yogi has to be very determined, patient and persistent.

# Verse 19

**bhavapratyayah videha prakrtilayanam**

bhava – inherent nature, psychology; pratyayah –mental content, objective awareness; videha- bodiless persons; prakritilayanam – of those who are diffused into subtle material nature

*Of those who are diffused into subtle material nature and those who existing in a bodiless state, their psychology has that content.*

## Commentary:

This is another jolt put to us by Sri Patanjali, as he explained why one yogi gets a certain advancement which is different from another and why without any current practice, some persons attain the benefits of yoga. In this case, those who are diffused into the subtle material nature without any effort on their part, without endeavor, are able to do so because of their inherent nature. A question remains as to whether this in the inherent nature of the spirit or of the psyche which is allied to it.

Sri Patanjali answered that question by throwing at us the word pratyaya, which means their mental content, the psychological make-up. However, even though it is not their spirits, still they have to adhere to that nature.

Certain other individuals attain the bodiless state and remain in material nature. They sometimes take birth but are unable to remain tied down to a material body due to their inherent tendency to be bodiless.

Bengali Baba, in his commentary on these sutras stated that the Videhas, the bodiless ones, are the persons who after performing virtuous actions such as Agnihotra ceremonies of the Vedas, attain the state of freedom, which is similar to absoluteness. He referred to Mandukopanisad, Chapter 2 Part 1. He wrote that they are not to return to human life but they will become presiding officers in future creations. He cited King Suratha who will be the eighth Manu after the reign of the current Manu who is Vaivasvata.

Such persons attain a permanent status as small-time gods of these worlds. They have no need at all to take a gross body. They either use a subtle body or no type of material body at all, but their energy affects this creation.

# Verse 20

sraddha virya smrti samadhiprajna purvakah itaresam

sraddha – confidence; virya –vigor, stamina; smrti – introspective memory; samadhi – continuous effortless linkage of the attention to a higher concentration force; prajna – profound insight; purvakah-previously practiced; itaresam – for others

*For others, confidence, stamina, introspective memory, the continuous effortless linkage of the attention to a higher concentration force, and profound insight, all being previously mastered, serves as the cause.*

## Commentary:

These are the requirements for those who want full success in attaining what Sri Patanjali described in the second sutra.

# Yogah cittavrtti nirodhah

**The skill of yoga is demonstrated by the conscious non-operation of the vibrational modes of the mento-emotional energy. (Yoga Sutra 1:2)**

One must have confidence in the practice of yoga and be satisfied with it to such an extent that one becomes attached to it above everything else and will do it to completion. If one does not have such confidence one will be stalled at the lower stages, one will give up the practice and take a position here or there in the material world, or one might become detached from gross existence but remain attached to certain subtle mundane life.

One must have stamina which arises with sufficient vigor to spur one to practice. There are many energies which contravene, or undermine yoga practice. If one does not have the stamina, one will be influenced by a negative force and will give up the practice.

One must practice samadhis repeatedly. Samadhi is the continuous effortless linkage of the attention to any of the higher concentration forces, which a yogi experiences . He must practice repeatedly.

The yogin must have profound insight gained through development of the buddhi intellect organ which sees beyond the material world into the super physical planes and beyond.

Sri Patanjali though acknowledging those person who are natural mystics, who can tune into the subtle material nature or who can exist in the material world in bodiless states, without having to do any yoga practice wrote these sutras expressly for those yogis who are endeavoring with such stamina that they will adhere to yoga, life after life until they reach the culmination.

There are many people who without any record of yoga practice in their current or perhaps even in their past lives, who are able to switch themselves to psychic or supernatural levels. But these persons rely on their inherent nature either to be accustomed to being bodiless, or to being diffused into particular subtle phases of material nature (prakrtilaya).

# Verse 21

tivrasamveganam asannah

tivra – very intense; samveganam – regarding those who practice forcibly; asannah - whatever is very near, what will occur soon

*For those who practice forcefully in a very intense way, the skill of yoga will be achieved very soon.*

## Commentary:

Even though Sri Patanjali stated that yoga is attained after a long time, he qualified that statemnt by saying that it is achieved shortly by those who have intense speedy practice. In fact one cannot conclude yoga practice in any life without intensity and persistence. It is impossible otherwise.

# Verse 22

mrdu madhya adhimatratvat tatah api visesah

mrdu – slight; madhya – mediocre; adhimatratvat - from intense; tatah - then; api = even; visesah - drating

*Then there is even more ratings, according to intense , mediocre, or slight practice.*

## Commentary:

Yoga practice yields results according to the intensity of correct practice. One person might practice intensely with the wrong methods. His result will be the realization of the incorrect practice. Another person might practice very little with the correct method but he too might not get the results because his practice does not have much forcefulness.

Sri Patanjali Maharshi gave four rates. Very intense (tivra-samvega), intense (adhimatratva), mediocre (madhya), and slight (mrdu).

# Verse 23

isvara pranidhanat va

isvara - The Supreme Lord; pranidhanat - derived from profound religious meditation; va - or

*Or by the method of profound religious meditation upon the Supreme Lord.*

## Commentary:

Sri Patanjali in an abrupt statement gave an alternative method (va -or), which is the profound religious meditation upon the Supreme Lord. Readers who want to inquire further into the meaning and application of this verse may check on the root words in Sanskrit to find out what that word *pranidhana* means. One should first check the root word dha, which meant to put, to lay upon, to fix upon, to hold, to contain, to seize. Then check nidhana, which means putting down, depositing, or a place where anything is placed. Then check pranidhana.

This indicates very profound and a deep laying of the mind upon the Supreme Lord. This is very deep meditation. If one can achieve that without doing yoga practice, one would be demonstrating that culmination of yoga , or one would have the mastery of yoga, even without practice.

# Verse 24

klesa karma vipaka asayaih aparamrstah purusavisesah isvarah

klesa – affliction, troubles; karma- action; vipaka- developments; asayaih – by subcounscious motivations; aparamrstah – unaffected; purusa – person; visesa – special; isvarah- Supreme Lord

*The Supreme Lord is that special person who is not affected by troubles, actions, developmens or by subconscious motivations.*

### Commentary:

Less there be no argument about it, Sri Patanjali clarified what he meant by the Supreme Lord, the Ishvara, as the person who is ever free from all afflictions, actions and developments in the material world and from subconscious motivations. Such a person wherever he may be found, would cause the devotee to enter into the higher consciousness for being free from the normal operations of the mento-emotional energy provided the devotee could do as instructed in the previous verse:

*isvara pranidhanat va* **"Or by the method of profound religious meditation upon the Supreme Lord." (Yoga Sutra 1:23)**

# Verse 25

tatra niratisayam sarvajnabijam

tatra – there, in Him; niratisayam – unsurpassed; sarvajna - all knowing; bijam – origin

*There, in Him, is found the unsurpassed origin of all knowledge.*

### Commentary:

This is a further description of the Supreme Lord. Sri Patanjali has carefully not named this Lord as Krishna or Shiva or Brahma, or anyone else. He gave that Lord's special characteristics through which He may be identified.

# Verse 26

sa esah purvesam api guruh kalena anavacchedat

sa =sah – He; esah – this particular person; purvesam – of those before, the ancient teachers; api – even; guruh – the spiritual teacher; kalena- by time; anavacchedat - unconditioned

*He, this particular person, being unconditioned by time is the guru even of the ancient teachers, the authorities from before.*

## Commentary:

In case there is doubt about this Supreme Person, Sri Patanjali informs us that He is the teacher even of the ancient authorities from before. He is ever existing and is ever the supreme master and supreme teacher of everyone.

# Verse 27

**tasya vacakah pranavah tasya – of Ahim; vacakah- what is denoted or named; pranavah – the sacred syllable AUM (Om)**

*Of Him, the sacred syllable Aum (Om) is the designation.*

### Commentary:

Om is the standard designation given to the Supreme Being by the Vedic sages of who went beyond this world before. In the Bhagavad-gita, Sri Krishna identified Himself with this Aum (Om).

# Verse 28

tajjapah tadarthabhavanam

taj = tat - that sound = japah – murmering; tadarthabhabanam= tat =that +artha – value + bhavanam – with deep feelings

*That sound is repeated, murmured constantly for realizing it's meaning.*

## Commentary:

A whimsical repitition of Aum (Om) will not serve the purpose. The japa murmuring has to be done with deep feeling and intense concentration. This leads into a deeper state of mind and to a quietude in which reverberates the sounds which come in from the super-physical world. These sounds are the actual Aum (Om) and the yogi recognizes them after purifying his mento-emotional energy through pranayama and a lack of interest in the material world.

A key factor is to disengage the gears of memory from the engine of the buddhi organ. For so long as the memory runs on automatically, the yogi cannot be free from the chatter and picturizations of the mind. Thus he will not experience what comes from the super-physical and spiritual world.

# Verse 29

tatah pratyakcetana adhigamah api antaraya abhavah ca

tatah – thence  what is resulting; pratyak – backwards, inwards, in the opposite direction; cetana - sense consciousness; adhigamah – accomplishment; api –also; antarya – obstacle; abhavah – not existing; ca – and

*As a result there is inwardness of the sense consciousness and the disappearance of obstacles to progress.*

## Commentary:

The result of chanting Omkara is given here as the attainment of the stage of pratyak (pratyahara), which is the internalization of the sense consciousness. Usually this consciousness courses outward into the subtle and gross material world. If Aum (Om) is repeated properly, one may develop introspection so that the same outward going sense energy turns back and begins to flow inwards.

This causes conservation of psychological energy in the realms of thinking and feeling. Thus the mento-emotional energy is restrained and conserved. The yogi then gets a boost of pranic charge and experiences super-physical and spiritual realities. This leads into dharana practice which is the sixth stage of yoga.

As soon as one has mastered the internalization of the sense consciousness, many obstacles goes away, because one is lifted out of the dimension where such hindrances exist. One transcends them. The obstacles remain for others who have not advanced to that stage.

# Verse 30

**vyadhi styana samsaya pramada alasya avirati bhrantidarsana
alabdhabhumikatva anavasthitatvani cittaviksepah te antarayah**

**vyadhi – disease; styana – idleness; samsaya – doubt; pramada –
inattentiveness; alasya – lack of energy; avirati – proness to sensuality;
bhrantidarsana- mistaken views; alabdhabhumikatva - not being
able to maintain the progress made, not holding the ground (bhumi);
anavasthitatvani – unsteadiness in the progression; cittaviksepah-
scattered mental and emotional energy; te – these; antaryah – obstacles**

*These obstacles are disease, idleness, doubt, inattentiveness, lack of energy
and prone to sensuality, mistaken views, not being able to maintain the
progress attained, unsteadiness in progression, scattered mental and
emotional energy.*

## Commentary:

Pratyahar practice which was described in the previous verse as being the
main benefit from the murmuring of the Aum (Om) sound, is the turning point
in the practice of a yogi. If he masters that, there is really no turning back form
him.  He will thereafter consolidate the progress.  Those who do not master
pratyahar are subjected to numerous types of discouragement in yoga practice.
It is mainly because they did not master pranayama.

Under a false notion (bhrantidarsana), a neophyte gets an idea that he does
not have to do any painstaking strenuous pranayama. Thus he neglects a very
important stage and is unable to change out the lower pranic energies in his
subtle body.

Let me go over the obstacles one by one.

### Disease (vyadhi)

Disease is an obstacle to any yogi who acquires a gross body for the practice
of yoga. That body is our means of deliverance but if it is unhealthy, our minds
and emotions will be disturbed in such a way as to cause us to desist from
practice for sometime. However a yogi should be realistic. He is a limited
being and he should not expect that his human form will always be free from
disease.

Some yogis, the advanced ones, maintain the practice even with disease.
This is to maintain the habit of the practice. If one passes on from a diseased
body and does not attain liberation, one will carry to the next human body the
tendency to do yoga, which will be an asset in the new form. Thus even if there
is disease, a yogin should maintain

whatever portion of the practice he can do with the diseased form.

One who has passed the seventh stage of yoga, that of dhyana effortless linkage of the attention to the higher concentration forces, is not put down by disease, but others definitely are. Since one's liberation is reliant on the status of one's human body, one should do as much as possible to protect the body from disease.

## Laziness / Idleness (styana)

 By constitution some persons do not have much determination. Their minds are fickle. Such persons come to a yoga class for quick liberation. Without understanding the requirement, they adopt the view that everyone can attain liberation in a jiffy or that a great yogin should be able to liberate everybody.

The truth is that everyone cannot become liberated because by constitution some spirits do not have the gomsha or inner drive to work for liberation.

However a person who is by nature idle-minded might become liberated if his atmas or spirit is connected existentially to a great yogin. By proximity to that great yogin, an idle-minded person might become liberated. If a boat has got too small of an engine, then a tug which is a small boat with an overly-powerful engine can pull it along. Similarly if another boat has a large enough engine which is defectively operating, it too can be pulled by a powerful tug. It is a question of how long such a tug would pull the powerless boat. How long can a great yogi drag an idle-minded disciple of his.

Idle mindedness can be overcome after long long practice, especially in pranayama and pratyahar, which are breath infusion and sensual restraints. It is the outpouring of the sensual energies which cause a person to have a scattered mind. This is why in the last sutra, Sri Patanjali indicated that if one chants the Omkara one could develop internalization.

## Doubt (samsaya)

Doubt is removed by personal experience of spiritual truths. Such experience comes after persistent practice. Some student yogis are doubtful by instinct. Even after having a few experiences, they remain troubled about the aim of yoga. This stresses their minds and causes them to go slower in the progressions.

A doubtful student will leave the path unless he or she is sustained in the practice by the association of a great yogin.

## Inattentiveness( pramada)

This is related to idleness, and is based on innate tendencies having to do with the scattering energies of the mind. It is by mastery of pratyahar, the fifth stage of yoga, that this is achieved. Inattentiveness is a state of mind which is driven by certain types of pranic forces which latch on to a particular living entity. If he or she can change that pranic energy, taking in a more concentrated type, the inattentiveness goes away.

### *Lack of energy (alasya)*

In yoga one has to endeavor. If there is a lack of energy, there will be no progress.

### *Proness to sensuality (avirati)*

This is also driven by the type of pranic energy in the mind. Hence the need for pranayama and pratyahar practice to change the nature of the mind by changing the energy content. The mental and emotional energy which we use has certain inherent capabilities.

### *Mistaken views (bhrantidarsana)*

Mistaken views come about according to the status of the buddhi organ which is used for analyzing. That organ, regardless of its accurate or inaccurate deductions, is prone to receiving information from the senses. The senses in turn accept information in a prejudiced way, depending on the type of sensual energy used and on the basis which come up in the memory circuits.

Purification of the buddhi brings about a dismissal of the mistaken views and that process is called buddhi yoga which is described in detail in chapter two and three of the Bhagavad-gita.

One must purify the life force, the kundalini chakra, as well as all parts of the subtle body. One must be celibate by practicing the yoga austerities. Then the buddhi organ assumes a brighter glow and becomes capable to avoiding mistaken views. The sensual energies are purified by pranayama and pratyahar practice.

### *Not being able to maintain the progress made (alabdhabhumikatva)*

A person who takes to yoga and who by association with a great yogi, makes some progress, may not be able to maintain the advancement. He or she might digress into a lower stage after some time. This is due to the assertion of the lower nature. It is due also to the distractions which come by virtue of the power of the memory. Instead of shedding off previous negative tendencies, the person is motivated by these, because of the probing and prompting of the memory circuits. Thus the person becomes distracted from yoga and is driven to live a life which is similar to the one used by non-yogis. Thus whatever progress is made is lost for the time being, when the lower tendencies take over the psyche and force it to their way of operation.

### *Unsteadiness in progress (anavasthitatvani)*

Unsteadiness in progression occurs because of the force of cultural activities. These acts force their way into the life of an aspiring yogi and cause him to abandon yoga altogether or to see it as being a side feature. When the cultural activities assert themselves as the priority, the yogi is unable to maintain a consistent practice. His progression becomes sporadic and he loses faith in yoga, thinking that it will not give him the results intended.

A yogi in such a position needs to consult with a person who understandings karma yoga as it is taught in the Bhagavad-gita to Arjuna. If one works under the direction of the Universal Form in helping with His duties in karma yoga, then one can ultimately be free from cultural acts, even from those which are enforced in this world by the Universal form of Sri Krishna. But one must be directed by a great yogi or alternately by Lord Shiva, Lord Balarama, or Lord Krishna.

### Scattered mental and emotional energy (cittaviksepah)

There is only one way to get rid of the scattered mental and emotional energy. That is the method of pranayama and pratyahar practice. Pratyahar practice causes one not to need much association from others because by it one conserves the sensual powers and enriches oneself being less and less dependent on whimsical social associations. Pranayama practice makes the yogin see that is is possible to change out the lower pranic energies in the psyche for higher ones which accelerate yoga.

# Verse 31

duhkha daurmanasya angamejayatva svasaprasvasah viksepa sahabhuvah

duhka –distress; daurmanasya – of mental depression; angame jayatva – nervousness of the body; svasaprasvasah – labored breathing; viksepa – distraction; sahabhuva – occurring with the symptoms

*Distress, depression, nervousness and labored breathing are the symptoms of a distracted state of mind.*

## Commentary:

Physical distress, mental distress, emotional distress causing nervousness of the body and labored breathing, occur as symptoms of a distracted mind. These manifest in old age as a matter of course. To decrease these occurances consistent asana and pranayama practice is required.

These distractions and the obstacles mentioned in the previous verse must be avoided by a yogin. He must recognize how these come about and stay away from their causes. He must know how to sidestep the human association which bring on or aggravate these.

# Verse 32

tatpratisedhartham ekatattva abhyasah

tat – that; pratidedha – removal; artham – for the sake of; eka – one; tattva- standard method in pursuit of reality (tattva); abhyasah – practice

*For the removal of the obstacles, there should be the practice of a standard method used in the pursuit of the reality.*

## Commentary:

One has no alternative but to practise, using methods which yogis in the past were successful in applying. Each yogin has to use a method that applies to his state of development. In the Bhagavad-gita also there is a similar statement about the practice:

*sri bhagavan uvaca*

*asamsayam mahabaho mano durnigraham calam*

*abhyasena tu kaunteya vairagyena ca grhyate*

The Blessed Lord said; Undoubtedly, O powerful man, the mind is difficult to control. It is unsteady. By practice, however, O son of Kunti, by indifference to its responses, also, it is restrained. (Gita 6.35)

# Verse 33

maitri karuna mudita upeksanam sukha duhkha punya apunya
visayanam bhavanatah cittaprasadanam

**maitri – friendliness; karuna – compassion; mudita- joyfulness, cheerfulness; upeksanam – indifference, neutrality, non- responsiveness; sukha – happiness; duhkha – distress; punya – virtue; apunya- vice; visayanam – relating to attractive objects; bhavantah – abstract meditation; citta-mento-emotional energy; prasadanam - serenity**

*The abstract meditation resulting from the serenity of the mento-emotional energy comes about by friendliness, compassion, cheerfulness and non-responsivness to happiness, distress, virtue and vice.*

## Commentary:

This reverts back to the second verse where the skill of yoga is defined:

# yogah cittavrtti nirodhah

"The skill of yoga demonstrated by the conscious non-operation of the vibrational modes of the mento-emotional energy." (Yoga Sutra 1:2)

The turbulence in the mental and emotional energies cause the living entity to be unsettled in the material creation and to strive after that which is temporary. This causes stress and ends in frustration, because the temporary manifested energy always changes either in a favorable or unfavorable way.

For stability of that energy, one has to practise yoga for a long time, but most persons are disinclined to the austerities and do not regard yoga as the priority. This is because they are given over to the sensual energies and the promises transmitted to them by such powers, promises that are not to be fulfilled in fact.

By cultivating friendliness, by administering compassion, by maintaining a cheerful demeanor and by an overall attitude of neutrality in non- responsivness to the movements of the lower energies, the yogin develops serenity of nature, which allows him to practice the abstract meditation through which he is allowed to break away from here and enter into the superphysical and spiritual dimensions.

# Verse 34

pracchardana vidharanabhyam va pranasya

prachardana – exhalation; vidharanabhyam – by inhalation; va – or;
pranasya –of the vital energy

*Or by regulating the exhalation and inhalationi of the vital energy*

## Commentary:

This is the practice of pranayama, the fourth statge of yoga practice. This must be learned from a knowlegable yogin who practices and knows the benefits of the methods he teaches. It may be discovered by a few fortunate students of yoga.

# Verse 35

visayavati va pravrttih utpanna manasah sthiti nibandhani

visayavati – like normal sensuality, something different but similar to a normal object; va – or; pravrttih – the operation; utpanna – produced, brought about; manasah – of the mind; sthiti- steadiness; nibandhani – bond, fusion

*Or fusion and steadiness of the mind is produced by the operation of the mento-emotional energy towards an object which is different to but similar to a normal thing.*

## Commentary:

This refers to the superphysical and or spiritual perception which is developed in the psyche of a yogi, especially in his buddhi organ through the curbing of the imagination faculty. Then the yogi sees objects which are not of the gross and subtle material energy but which are superphysical and spiritual. Perceiving such objects brings steadiness of mind and fusion of the attention of the yogi into the higher level of reality, the chit akash.

Visaya is a normal sense object of this world, something to which our normal senses are usually attracted to either for attaching itself or for repulsing itself from. Vati means something that is similar, something like that. Objects in the sky of consciousness are also objects but they do not cause the self to be degraded as the objects in this world do.

The term pravritti means operation, for active function. Even though the mastership of yoga is to the stop the conventional operation of the mental and emotional energies, still this means that they must be stopped on this side of existence. Hence the functioning of that energy for perception of spiritual objects causes the fusion of the mental- emotional force to a higher reality.

# Verse 36

visokah va jyotismati

**visokah – sorrow-less; va – or; jyotismati – spiritually luminous**

*Or by sorrowless and spiritual luminous states*

### Commentary:

The experience of various student yogis differ, but the similarity is that the experiences cause them to have faith in the practice of yoga, and it increases their drive for progress. It is not stereo-typed. One person might see beyond this physical world into the sky of consciousness. Another might feel a sorrowless energy or experience sheer spiritual light.

Any of these experiences which are valid alternatives to this subtle and gross material existence, will result in the stability of mind required to put a halt to the operations of the mental and emotional energy, thus leading to personal experiences of the transcendence, and to mastership of one's interaction with this material world.

# Verse 37

vitaraga visayam va cittam

vita – without; raga – craving; visayam -an object or person; va – or; cittam – mento-emotional energy

*Or fixing the mento- emotional energy on someone who is without craving.*

## Commentary:

One may, by association with a great yogi who is free from craving develop stability to stop the razzy dazzy operations of the mental and emotional energies. Such associations can definitely cause this.

# Verse 38

svapna nidra jnana alambanam va

svapna – dream; nidra – dreamless sleep; jnana – information; alambanam- taking recourse; va - or

*Or by taking recouse to dream or dreamless sleep*

## Commentary:

Some yogis gain steadiness of mental and emotional energy by keeping track of their dreams and by remaining objectively conscious in dreamless sleep. Through these mystic observations they study the movements of consciousness and are able to discern reality and non-reality and to situate themselves in the state which is detached from the normal operations of the mental and emotional force. For success in this course a yogi must distance himself from his memory, because its impressions aggravate the instability of the mind and motivate the emotional energies to create picture sensations for further cultural activity in the material world.

# Verse 39

yathabhimata dhyanat va

yatha – as, according; abhimata – what is dearly desired; dhyanat – from effortless linkage of the mind to a higher concentration force; va – or

*Or it can be achieved from the effortless linkage of the mind to a higher concentration force which was dearly desired.*

## Commentary:

This gives the hint that through love and endearment, one may attain the cessation of the undesirable operations of the mental and emotional energy. The process of bhakti or devotion is mentioned in this verse under the term abhimata which means agreeable, beloved and endearing.

# Verse 40

**paramanu paramamahattvantah asya vasikarah**

paramanu = paprama – smallest + atom; parama – greatest; mahatva – largeness, cosmic proportions;

antah – ending, extending to; asya – of his, him; vasikarah – mastery of the psyche

*The mastery of his psyche results in control of his relationship to the smallest atom or to cosmic proportions.*

## Commentary:

Some commentators explain that this means the yogi gains control over what is atomic (anu) and what is cosmic (mahatva). However on a close check of the Sanskrit term vasikarah, this does not tally with what Sri Patanjali indicated. He means that the yogi is able to control not the atomic and cosmic but rather his relationship to the same. By controlling the forces in his psyche, his psychological energies, he acquires a greater degree of control over his response to what is cosmic and atomic. Those aspects remain the same in the universe he inhabits, but his response to them changes in such a way as to set him in a position of relative immunity to their negative or spiritually detrimental influences. This occurs because of the yogin's detachment, his lack of interest as described in text 12 and 15.

While a human being is almost compelled to react in a preset way to a set of circumstances or to a type of energy, the yogin, because he has switched his energy intake to a higher concentration force, can side-step most influences and remain in an unbiased status as conferred on him by his yoga practice.

# Verse 41

ksinavrtteh abhijatasya iva maneh grahitr grahana grahyesu tatstha
tadanjanata samapattih

ksina – great reduction; vrtteh – concerning the mento-emotional
operations; abhijatasya – of what is produced all around or transparent;
iva –like; maneh – of a gem; grahitr- perceiver; grahana – flow perception;
grahyesu – in what is perceived; tatstha – basis foundation; tad = tat-
that; anjanata – assuming the nature of or characterization of (anj- to
smear with, to mix with); samapattih – linkage fusion.

*In regards to the great reduction of the mento-emotional operations, there
is fusion of the perceiver, the flow of perceptions and what is perceived,
just like the absorption of a transparent jewel.*

## Commentary:

This happens also in ordinary experiences, when a person becomes totally
preoccupied as it were with gross objects or an endearing feeling. Thus what
is as special about a yogin who achieves this after much practice at greatly
reducing the impulsive operations of his mento-emotional energy.

There must be a difference in the accomplishment of the yoga. For one thing,
the ordinary person is driven impulsively. He has not practiced to stop the
automatic operations of his mental and emotional energies. He has no control
over the fusion of his consciousness with various forces to which his mind
and emotions are impulsively attracted. He does not have to purify in psyche
which the yogi earned by higher yoga practice. The yogin's linkage with
higher concentration forces is quite different to the ordinary man's absorption
with subtle and gross energy which is perceived by an impure psyche.

# Verse 42

tatra sabda artha jnana vikalpaih sankirna savitarka samapattih

**tatra** – there, in that case; **sabda** – word; **artha**- meaning; **jnana** – knowledge concerning something; **vikalpaih** – with option, alternative, doubt , uncertainty; **sankirna** – blending together, mixed; **savitarka** – thoughtfulness, reasoning, deliberation; **samapattih** – fusion linkage

*In that case, the deliberate linkage of the mento-emotional energy to a higher concentrating force occurs when a word, its meaning and the knowledge of the object alternate within the mind, blending as it were.*

## Commentary:

There are various types of linkage between the yogin's partially or fully purified attention and some other person or force. It might be a person or force residing in his psyche or one that is exterior to it. When that linkage occurs with the analytical organ being operative, then it is called deliberative linkage or vitarka samapattih. Sri Patanjali defined each type of higher linkage to clarify the various levels of accomplishment of a yogi and to remove any vagueness regarding lower accomplishment and higher yoga.

# Verse 43

**smrtiparisuddhau svarupasunya iva arthamatranirbhasa nirvitarka**

**smrti – memory; parisuddhau – on complete purification; svarupa–essential nature of something; sunya – devoid of; iva – as if; artha – meaning; matra – only; nirbhasa – shining; nirvitarka – fusion or linkage without deliberation of analysis.**

*Non-analytical linkage of his attention to a higher concentration force occurs when the memory is completely purified and the essential inquiring nature disappears as it were, such that the value of that higher force shines through.*

### Commentary:

This is a description of what a yogi experiences when he engages in non-analytical linkage of his attention to a higher concentration force with a purified memory and when he find that the analytical urges of the buddhi organ cease functioning. Then he discovers the value of the higher concentration force or person to which he is linked.

Readers should not get frustrated because these are very complicated explanations given by Sri Patanjali. After all, what he describes has to do with very subtle superphysical and spiritual phenomena. This is not easy to understand. It gives us an appreciation of the accomplishments of the great yogins.

Shudda means purity but pari shudda means complete, all around purity. When the memory is cleaned by a consistent and thorough practice which results in stopping it's impulsive activations and silencing its influences and biases, then the yogi is able to disarm the buddhi organ. This is the important clue in this verse.

Because the buddhi carries the weapon of analysis, it is able to blackmail and intimidate the self into cooperating with the plan of the impulsive but blind life force and the sensible but shortsighted senses. Thus when the yogin silences the weapon of analysis, he becomes freed from its harassments.

At that time the senses become powerless to bother him, because they lose the protective support of their powerful friend, the analytical intellect organ (buddhi). Thus the yogin no longer has to fight with the memory to stop it from whimsically and impulsively showing him so many impressions on their visual and audial forms. With such distractions reduced to nil, he progresses quickly and is able to move his attention into the realm of the chit akash, the sky of consciousness.

# Verse 44

etayaiva savicara nirvicara ca suksmavisaya vyakhyata

etaya – by this; eva – only; savicara – investigative linkage of one's attention to a higher concetration force; nirvicara – non-investigative linkage; ca – and; suksma – subtle; visaya – object; vyakhyata – explained

*By this, the investigatative linkage and non- investigative linkage of one's attention to a higher concentration force consisting of subtler objects, was explained.*

## Commentary:

There is a difference between an analytical linkage and an investigative one. There is a slight difference. It depends on the yogi's interest in particular subtle phenomenea as well as on the influence of the higher concentration force to which he is linked. At a higher stage, he regards the subject of interest without the bias of analytical or investigative approach. This is called surrender to the higher concentration force, person or thing as well as to his relationship with it.

# Verse 45

suksmavisayatvam ca alinga paryavasanam

suksma – subtle; visayatvam – what is concerning the nature of gross objects; ca – and; alinga - without characteristics; paryavasanam – termination

*The insight into the subtle nature of gross objects, terminates when one becomes linked to the higher concentration force which has no characteristics.*

## Commentary:

As far as matter is concerned, a yogin has to research into it by linking his attention to its subtle states. Ultimately, he will reach a stage where he connects with the undifferentiated status of matter which is it's ultimate stage. At that point, his research into it terminates. Yet he still has to discover the role played by the Supreme Lord

(Ishvar) in activating and manifesting matter.

Sri Patanjali has graciously informed all student-yogins that when they reach the featureless state of the subtle material energy, they have reached the end of their research into it. But this must be discovered by each yogin during the linkage of his attention to higher concentration forces.

# Verse 46

ta eva sabijah samadhih

ta- they; eva – only; sabijah – with motivation from the mento-emotional energy; samadhih- effortless continous linkage of the attention to a higher concentration force

*The previous descriptions concern the effortless and continuous linkage of the attention to a higher concentration force, as motivated by the mento-emotional energy.*

## Commentary:

After making so much progress in higher yoga, a yogin realizes that what he was engaged in, was being motivated by the same mental and emotional energy which he endeavored to transcend. This is because he discovered that besides himself there was a force in his psyche which derived fulfillments from the endeavors. He traces and discovers that these were a psychic motivational force which derived a pleasure from his practice.

At that stage the practice begins in earnest and the purpose of the material energy in the life of the yogi is revealed. Bowing to the mental and emotional mundane energy in his psyche he moves on in appreciation. The purpose for which the Supreme Being caused the limited self, His eternal partner, to come in contact with a mundane life force and an investigative organ called a buddhi, now become evident to the yogin.

# Verse 47

nirvicara vaisaradye adhyatmaprasadah

nivicara = non – investigative linkage of one's attention to a higher concentration force; vaisaradye – on gaining competence; adhyatma – relationship between the supreme soul and the limited one; prasadah – clarity and serenity

*On gaining competence in the non-investigative linkage of one's attention to the higher concentration force, one experiences the clarity and serenity which results from the linkage of the supreme soul and the limited one.*

## Commentary:

When the yogin passes beyond the realm of material nature, his attention links up with spiritual energy in total. Then he may, if he continues to progress, gain the competence described in this verse. That causes his limited spirit to link up with the Supreme personality. From that connection a serenity of spirit as well as a clarity of the relation between him and that Supreme person develops.

# Verse 48

rtambhara tatra prajna

**rtambhara – reality – perceptive, truth discerning; tatra – there, at that time; prajna – insight**

*There with that competence, the yogin develops the reality-perceptive insight.*

### Commentary:

The rtambhara buddhi is called by different terms elsewhere in the Vedic literatures like the Bhagavad-Gita. It is termed as jnana-dipena and jnana chaksusa. This means the lighted (dipena) insight (jnana) or the vision (chaksusa) of insight (jnana). In yoga parlance it is sometimes called the cleansed brow chakra, or third eye. However this comes after much practice, when the mental and emotional energy (citta) is silenced, when it stops vibrating in reference to the subtle and gross material energy and when it becomes stabilized and converts the imagination orb into exacting visual insight.

Srila Yogeshwara of Gangotri, that great yogin, rated this rtambhara buddhi highly. He recommended its development to all yogins. Sri Patanjali clarified that until one reaches the stage of nivicara Samadhi, that of non-investigative linkage of one's attention to a highter concentration force in the chit akash, one cannot develop this rtambhara buddhi. Patanjali identified the stage at which a yogin develops this.

# Verse 49

sruta anumana prajnabhyam anyavisaya visesarthatvat

sruta – what is heard; anumana – what is surmised or seasoned out; prajnabhyam- from the two methods of insight; anya – other; visaya – object; visesa – particular aspect; arthavat – because of an object

*It is different from the two methods of insight which are based on what is heard and what is reasoned out, because that is limited to a particular aspect of an object.*

## Commentary:

Direct perception with the reality-perceptive insight is different to conventional perception which is based on what is heard or read of and what is surmised or reasoned out on the basis of lower sense perception. This is because in lower sense perception, the mind can only deal with one aspect at a time. It then presents this to the buddhi organ for analysis and comparison. Then through prejudiced notions one forms opinions. This is haphazard.

# Verse 50

ajjah samskarah anyasamskara pratibandhi

taj= tat- that; jah- which is produced from; samskarah- the impressions; anya- other; samkara- impression; pratibandhi- the preventer, that which effectively suppresses something else

*That impression which is produced from the reality-perceptive insight, acts as the preventer of the other impressions.*

## Commentary:

Sri Patanjali's Sanskrit language and dissection of yoga practice is precise. Let us say for example that a car shifts into second gear at 25 miles per hour. The driver might never realize the fact, however, the engineer who designed the transmission or another observant person would know of the 25 mile per hour speed shifting requirement. Some persons who have mastered higher yoga to a degree are to an extent ignorant of the details of higher yoga practice. Unfortunately some of these persons took up the task of translating and commenting on these sutras. They gave opinions that are at variance with what Patanjali intended.

Sri Patanjali composed a Sanskrit grammar which means that he was very knowledgable of the language. To deal with his Sanskrit, one has to know Sanskrit grammar thoroughly. Patanjali was very observant of his own yoga practice and had good schooling in it. Besides he is a mahayogin from his previous births. Thus to translate and comment on his sutras is a challenge for anyone. In any case, he did use a great favor by showing up the stages of higher yoga, a process which to say the least, is vague even to many of the yogins who reached the higher practice. This is because of the subtlety of the experiences and the failure of yogins to observe the minute details as Sri Patanjali did. By a careful study of the information, any yogi can get some idea of where he is located on the path.

Sri Patanjali informed us, that the impression derived from the reality-perceptive insight acts as a preventer to the other impressions in the psyche which were formed by the lower buddhi organ and which bother a student yogi.

This information is significant, because in higher yoga one wonders when and where, one will get rid of the impressions which arise repeatedly in the mind and jar one lose from the prescribed focus. The answer is that until one develps the reality-perceptive insight as stipulated here, one will not able to completely suppress the distracting impressions. One will have to tolerate them to a degree and use other partial controlling methods. This clears misconceptions and gives the student yogi hope that a time will come when the bothersome memories will be suppressed.

# Verse 51

tasyapi nirodhe sarvanirodhat nirbijah samadhih

tasya - of that (preventative impression); api- also; nirodhe – on the non operation; sarva – all; nirodhat – resulting from that non-operation; nirbijah – not motivated by the mento-emotional energy; samadhi – continuous effortless linkage of the attention to the higher concentration force

*The continous effortless linkage of the attention to the higher concentration force which is not motivated by this mento-emotional energy, occurs when there is a non-operation, even of that preventative impression which caused the suppression of all other lower memories.*

### Commentary:

When all the impressions cease to be activated, when they all seem to be finished for good, then the highest contemplation occurs. That is a contemplation which is not motivated from this end of existence. It is controlled by and operated by the higher spiritual level of existence, from the other side of life, the chit akash.

Traditionally this first chapter is called Samadhi pada, which means the chapter defining Samadhi. The Second chapter is usually called sadhana pada, which deals with the practice of yoga. That is of special interest to the student yogis. After describing the higher yoga, the so-called raja yoga, Sri Patanjali described the practice of yoga as it is. Anyone who calls himself a yogi or aspires for that honor, should pay close attention to the second chapter.

# 2
# Sādhana-pāda
# (Practice)

The second chapter is about sadhana,"effective means of attainment", and refers to specific religious disciplines. The purpose of the practice is twofold—achieving samadhi and lessening the five wrong cognitions.

# Verse 1

**tapah-svadhyayesvara-pranidhanani kriya-yogah**

tapah – austerity; svadhyaya – study of the psyche; isvarapranhanani = isvara - Supreme Lord + pranidhanani – profound religious meditation; kriyayayoga – dynamic yoga practice

*Austerity, study of the psyche, profound religious meditation on the Supreme Lord is the dynamic kriya yoga practice.*

## Commentary:

There are many Vaishnava teachers who deride Sri Patanjali as an impersonalist. This is because they misunderstand these sutras and have a negative bias towards yoga. Even though Srila Vyasadeva, his son Shuka and others like Narada, themselves being leading Vaishnavas, did perfect the dynamic kriya yoga practice, still today many Vaishnava leaders who hail in their name, denounce the very process as being devoid of bhakti or devotion to Ishvara. Thus they ridicule it as being useless.

However it is clear that this dynamic kriya yoga - practice was taught to Uddhava by Sri Krishna in their final conversation. The three aspects mentions, namely austerity, (tapah) study of the psyche (svadhyaya) and profound religious meditation upon the Supreme Lord (Isvarapranidhanani) are absolutely essential for the liberation of a living being. Whether one cultivates this by long practice, as Sri Patanjali described or one does so effortlessly as Sri Caitanya MahaPrabhu did, it will still be necessary in one way or the other either ( text missing)…natural ability. There is no avoiding this. Ultimately it must be done.

Those who do the dynamic kriya practice and who avoid the profound religious meditation upon the Supreme Lord, must substitute a profound type of religious meditation toward the yogi guru who gives them techniques. Ultimately, the offering of devotion to that person reaches the Supreme Lord, either directly or through the chain of siddhas, who ultimately must be connected to that ultimate teacher, the spiritual master of the ancient yogis. The profound religious meditation cannot be avoided in the course of dynamic kriya yoga. This explains why someone may become a siddha even though he is not an avowed devotee of that Supreme Lord. It is because that person has an indirect but very effective connection to the Godhead.

# Verse 2

**samadhi-bhavanarthah klesa-tanu-karanarthas ca**

samadhi – continuous effortless linkage of the attention to a higher concentration force or person; bhavana – producing; arthah - for the value or purposes of; klesa = mento-emotional afflictions; tanu - thinking reducing; karana - cause, causing; arthas = arthah- for the value of purpose; ca – and

*It is for the purpose of producing continuous effortless linkage of the attention to a higher concentration force and for causing the reduction of the mental and emotional afflictions.*

**Commentary:**

Without the reduction of the mental and emotional afflictions, there can be no Samadhi or continuous effortless linkage of the attention to a higher concentration force or person. This is because the afflictions serves as effective distractions which keep the buddhi organ engaged in lower pursuits, effectively baring it from focusing into higher places of consciousness. The dynamic kriya yoga is necessary. It is the only process which systematically reduces the mental and emotional botherations and gradually puts the psyche at a distance from them. It does not postpone them nor put them into dormancy nor drown them out with sounds and picturations. It brings them to an end.

# Verse 3

**avidyasmita-raga-dvesabhinivesah klesah**

**avidya – spiritual ignorance; asmita – misplaced identity; raga – a tendency of emotional attachment; dvesa - impulsive emotional disaffection; abhinivesah – strong focus on mundane existence which is due to an instinctive fear of death; klesah – the mental emotional afflictions**

*The mental and emotional afflictions are spiritual ignorance, misplaced identity, emotional attachment, impulsive emotional disaffection and the strong focus on mundane existence, which is due to an instinctive fear of death.*

### Commentary:

The prime cause of the mental and emotional afflictions is spiritual ignorance (avidya). Unfortunately this ignorance is primeval for many of the living entities who end up in the material creation. They have no idea of their spiritual whereabouts. They assume that their existence is mundane. By not understanding their essential self (sva-bhava), they are subjected to endless mis-identities, on and on and on. It is by the grace of a guru that one gets some idea about the essential self. It is by the example of a guru that one makes the endeavor to release the self.

The misplaced self identity (asmita) causes numerous afflictions in the day to day existence. By it, one attaches one's psychological energy to persons and things in a harmful way. It is by yoga discipline that one develops the power to control the sense of identity, so that it may focus only on higher realities and ultimately cause one to be situated in a permanent non-painful condition.

The tendency for emotional attachment (raga) is an impulse which is curbed after one has mastered the pratyahar fifth stage of yoga practice, consisting of withdrawing the sensual energies from their external pursuits and conserving that energy within the psyche for application to higher realities.

The impulsive emotional disaffection occurs on the basis of justified or unjustified biases acquired in the present and past lives. It is impulsively performed and is hard to control. By higher yoga, one can bring this to an end.

The strong focus on mundane existence which is due to an instinctive fear of death (abhinivesah ) is removed by the realization of the self. One must gain mystic experiences whereby one finds oneself in one's subtle body when it is separated from the gross one. Gradually by repeated experiences of this sort, one loses the instinctive fear of death and finds that it is no longer necessary to maintain a strong focus on material existence, since one will definitely survive the perishable body. These five causes of the mental and emotional afflictions must be removed before one can enter Samadhi on a regular basis.

# Verse 4

avidya ksetram uttaresam prasupta-tanu-vicchina-udaranam

**avidya** – spiritual ignorance; **ksetram** - field, existential environment; **uttaresam** – of the other afflictions; **prasupta** – dormant; **tanu** – reducted; **vicchina** – alternating, periodic; **udaranam** – expanded

*Spiritual ignorance is the existential environment for the other afflictions, in their dormant, reduced, periodic or expanded stages.*

## Commentary:

Spiritual ignorance (avidya) is the root cause of the mental and emotional distresses which come upon a living entity, and which is perceived as an impediment by aspiring yogins. The other afflictions form on the basis of spiritual ignorance. These four others arise in the psychological environment of a person who is spiritually-ignorant of his self-identity, due to having not experienced it objectively and due to having a strong focus on gross existence.

# Verse 5

anityasuci-dukhanatmasu nitya-suci-sukhatmakhyatir avidya

anitya – not eternal, temporary; asuci - not clean, not pure; duhkha – distress; anatmasu – in what is not the spirit; nitya – eternal; suci – pure; sukha – happiness; atma – spirit; khyatih - what is known or identified; avidya- spiritual ignorance

*Spiritual ignorance is exhibited when what is temporary, impure, distressful and mundane, is identified as being eternal, pure, joyful and spiritual respectively.*

### Commentary:

This exhibition is rooted in the strong focus on gross existence which is due to an instinctive fear of death (abhinivesah, verse 3) by that focus one mistakes what is temporary, feeling that it is or can be permanent, if it is maintained by one's interest in it. One feels that what is impure can be purified by external means and by decorations. One does not recognize what is distressful but instead feels that it is joy-yielding. One mistakes what is not the spirit for the spirit. For example, one feels that one's body is oneself, and that it might be possible for one to live as the body forever.

# Verse 6

**drg-darsana-saktyor ekatmatevasmita**

drg = drk - supernatural vision; darsana – what is seen; saktyoh - of the two potencies; ekatmata – having one nature, identical; iva – as if, seems to be; asmita- mistaken identity

*Mistaken identity occurs when the supernatural vision and what is seen through it seems to be identical.*

### Commentary:

The drg shakti or drk shakti is the supernatural visionary power which emits from the spirit itself. It is not what is seen, even though it is the medium which is used directly or in the conjunction with other perceiving instruments. Hence it is mistaken identity when one feels that what is seen is identical to his own vision.

First of all, the supernatural vision is experienced as one's attention on this level of existence. On this level one uses a subtle and gross instrument for focusing one's attention. The subtle instrument is the buddhi which is the brain of the subtle body. The gross instrument is the brain, and it's auxiliary nerves. When the attention is focused through the subtle reality, it suffers from inaccuracy. Therefore it is a mistake to think that it is true vision or direct perception.

# Verse 7

**sukhanusayi ragah**

**sukha – happiness; anusayi – connected to, devotedly attached to; ragah – craving**

*Craving results from a devoted attachment to happiness*

## Commentary:

A yogin must study his own psychology to see how it operates.. He should take steps to curb it for success in yoga. Every yogi is required to pay attention to his own nature, to find its defects and to alter it in the interest of progress.

Human nature develops cravings by being devotedly attached to happiness. Happiness is derived from sensual contact in terms of smelling, tasting, seeing, touching and hearing. In the pratyahar sensual withdrawal stages, a yogi gets to understand how he becomes attached to various types of happiness and how his attachments develops into craving, which forms compulsive habits. Each yogi must systematically review his own conduct to understand this. Then he should correct himself.

# Verse 8

### dukhanusayi dvesah

**duhkha – distress; anusayi – connected to, devotedly attached to; dvesah-impulsive emotional disaffection**

*Impulsive emotional disaffection results from a devoted attachment to distress.*

## Commentary:

Impulsive emotional disaffection is manifest as an instinctive dislike for something or someone. One can become habituated to such disaffection. This results in a cynical attitude and an abhorrence towards one object or the other. It destroys yoga practice.

Distress, though painful on the emotional level, may be liked by someone. Thus the person is drawn into distressful situations again and again to derive the emotional satisfaction causes by linking the emotions to painful situations. All this should be discovered by a yogin, so that he can wean himself from distress and its causes.

# Verse 9

svarasa-vahi viduso' pi tatha rudho bhinivesah

svarasavahi = sva - own + rasa – essence + vahi – flow current, instinct for self preservation(svarasavahi - it's own flow of energy of self preservation); vidus = vidusah – the wise man; 'pi – api – also; tatha – just as, so it is; rudho – rudhah - developed produced; 'bhinivesah = abhinivesah – strong focus on mundane existence which is due to instinctive fear of death

*As it is, the strong focus on mundane existence, which is due to the instinctive fear of death, and which is sustained by its own potencies, which operates for self preservation, is developed even in the wise man*

## Commentary:

Even though wise, a person has to curb his instinctive life force. This is why the mastership of kundalini yoga is necessary before one can attain salvation. It is due to the natural sense of self preservation, which is present in the subtle body, which is instinctively fearful of not having a gross form and of having to leave such a form permanently.

Unless on effectively resists the life force in the subtle body, his wisdom or knowledge can do nothing to remove the strong fear of death. The resistance is acquired by intake of higher pranic energies, through pranayama and other methods which form parts of the kriya yoga practice..

Mastery of the life force, the kundalini chakra, gives the yogin the ability to infuse the subtle body with a lack of fear, due to its conscious experiences in the subtle world. When the subtle body takes a footing in the subtle existence it releases itself from dependence on this gross manifestation, and the fear of death (abhinivesah) departs from it.

In his translation, the Raj Yogi I.K. Taimni gave riding and dominating as the meaning of rudhah. His translation reads that abhinivesa is the strong desire for life which dominates even the learned (or the wise). In his purport, he stated that the universality of abhinivesah shows that there is some constant and universal force inherent in life which automatically find expression in this "desire to live".

In higher yoga one realizes this when one traces that urge to the life force in the subtle body and then to the cosmic life force which dominates or rides on the back of the psyche, dictating by urges and motivations, how it should procure gross existences, maintain these and fight to remain rooted in these.

It is only when a yogin has developed a yoga siddha body that he becomes totally free of that life force impulse which forces him to procure a foot hole in the gross existences for participation in the struggle for survival in lower worlds.

# Verse 10

te pratiprasava-heyah suksmah

te – these, they; prati – opposing, reverting back; prasava- expressing, going outwards; heyah- what is fit to be left or abandoned; suksmah – subtle energies

*These subtle motivations are to be abandoned by reverting their expressions backwards.*

### Commentary:

This means the practice of raja yoga or mystic actions which effectively curb and end off what is unwanted in the psyche and what deters the objectives of yoga.

Pratiprasava is known otherwise as the fifth stage of yoga which is pratyahara (pratiahara) reverting the sensual expressions back into the psyche, so that they do not express themselves outwards. This causes conservation of valuable psychic energy through which one develops supernatural perception.

There are many subtle motivations which are quite fit to be abandoned or left aside, to be made powerless so that they do not motivated the psyche of the yogi in a counter productive way. However one must develop the power to shut down or squelch such energies, otherwise one can say what he likes and believe whatever suits his fancy and he will still be motivated by these energies to his detriment.

# Verse 11

**dhyana-heyas tad-vrttayah**

**dhyana - effortless linking of the attention to the higher concentration force or person; heyah – what is fit to be abandoned or left aside; tad = tat-that; vrttayah - vibrational modes of the mento-emotional energies**

*Their vibrational modes are to be abandoned or ceased by the effortless linkage of the attention to a higher concentration force or person.*

## Commentary:

This advice is direct. It does not state that there are alternate methods for dealing with the vibrational motivations which spring from the abhinivesha urges which cause a yogi and others to pursue mundane life with a wanton passion which usually cannot be controlled. This is because there are no other methods but the attempt at effortless linkage of the attention to higher concentration forces or persons. This is the only method that reveals to the yogin the various parts of the psyche and the complications he faces in trying to purify his nature. The vibrational modes which apply to the lower psychic level and to the physical planes, are not to be silenced except by causing the mind to abandon those lower planes. The techniques are realized by practicing higher yoga.

# Verse 12

## klesa-mulah karmasayah drstadrsta-janma-vedaniyah

**klesa** –mento emotional distress; **mulah** – root – cause ; **karma**- cultural activities ; **asayah**- storage, reservoir; **drsta**- perceived, realized; **adrsta**- not perceived, not realized; **janma** – birth; **vedaniyah** – what is experienced or realized

*The psychological storage of the impressions left by performance of cultural activities which is itself the cause of the mental and emotional distress, is experienced in realized and non-realized births.*

### Commentary:

This karma asayah or psychological storage-compartment which holds the compacted impressions which are left by the performance of cultural activities, is manifested to us in meditation as memory. It is very troublesome and stalls the yogi in his attempts to master pratyahar, dharana and dhyana. A yogi may be stalled for years by motivations which come out of the memory compartment. When the memory emits impressions, they are translated when they hit the mento-emotional energy, the citta. Then the buddhi organ takes possession of the pictures and sounds and creates further impressions, causing the psyche to create desires and motivations to act. This is the bane of higher yoga. Until a yogin can control this, he does not progress in the dharana and dhyana practice.

Some translators have innocently translated drsta adrsta janma as present and future births, but this is a mistake. Drsta does not mean what is present in terms of time and adrsta does not mean what is not present today. Drsta means observing or seeing, perceiving. Adrsta is the opposite meaning births that do not objectively realize. In other words, in some births one can realize that it is a temporary circumstance one has entered into and in other births due to limited perception one does not realize this. As for instance, in the case of souls who take animal or vegetative forms. They have no idea that they are in a birth for a limited amount of time. Still, as Sri Patanjali stated, the person will experience the impressions which were in his psyche, and which were left behind by his past acts in the cultural worlds. He cannot avoid those experiences even though he may not make any sense of why the impressions go through his mind.

The impressions are experienced even by animals and trees but they do not understand what they perceive. The spiritually-ignorant human beings do not understand the impression either. They try to rationalize all of it in terms of what they remember in the present life. A yogi, by higher practice, has a big advantage, because according to his level of advancement, he may understand the impressions to a lesser or greater degree. He may also get help from his teachers, who are conversant with the forces in the psyche.

# Verse 13

sati mule tad-vipako jaty-ayur-bhogah

sati- there is existing; mule – in the cause; tat – that, it; vipakah – what is resulting; jati – species, status of life; ayuh – duration of life; bhogah- type of experience

*In the case aforementioned, there exists the resulting effects which manifest as a particular species of life with certain duration of body and type of experiences gained in that form.*

## Commentary:

One develops a certain type of body with a duration for it's existence along with the experience gained through that form, on the basis of the impressions which were formed before the performance of cultural activities. All species of life are engaged in cultural acts. The human is more deliberate. This is his only advantage. Even though on forgets the cultural acts from past lives still one's life is to a greater degree, determined by the type of cultural acts one performed previously. The psychological storage compartment holds the impressions of the past cultural acts, as motivations to take advantage of certain situations. This is done impulsively.

# Verse 14

te hlada-paritapa-phalah punyapunya-hetutvat

**te- they; hlada- happiness; paritapa- distress; phalah- results; punya – merits; apunya- demerits; hetutvat – that which causes**

*They produce happiness and distress as results, on the basis of merit and demerits.*

## Commentary:

The impressions from previous cultural activities form happy or unhappy times according to the laws of nature, not according to what human beings believe. The rationalization of human beings, particularly the fundamental religious ones, do not necessarily tally with the laws of nature.

The merits are those which are approved by nature. The demerits form from Her disapproval. However, a living being must sometimes wait for many years, or even many thousands of years before he can enjoy or suffer for breaking or confirming to a law of nature.

His past cultural acts which left impressions in his subconscious memory (karmasayah) remains there until it senses a favorable circumstance from its meritorious or demeritorious reaction.

# Verse 15

parinama-tapa-samskara-dukhair guna-vrtti-virodha ca dukhameva
sarvam vivekinah

parinama -circumstantial change; tapa - strenuous endeavor; samskara -
impulsive motivations; duhkhaih - with distress; guna - quality, features
of material nature; vrtti - vibrational mode of the mento-emotional
energy; virodhat - resulting from confrontation or clashing aspects; ca
- and; duhkham – distress; eva – indeed; sarva - all; vivekinah – the
discriminating person

*The discriminating person knows that all conditions are distressful because
of circumstantial changes, strenuous endeavor, impulsive motivations,
clashing aspects and the vibrational modes of the mento-emotional energy.*

## Commentary:

This is discrimination gained by virtue of yoga practice. It is an insight into
the nature of the material world and is not a theoretical understanding of it. By
this, a yogi sees the complications in the cultural activities. Thus he becomes
reluctant to participate. One cannot control the features of material nature.
If one does not advance into higher yoga, one cannot control the vibrational
modes of one's mental and emotional energies.

Therefore a yogi has no alternative but to back away from the cultural world
and harden-up himself by performing higher yoga, mastering it and then
applying it while performing any remaining cultural obligations efficiently,
and in a way that causes a breaking off from the cultural circuit.

The conditions in these lower existences, are always distressful either in the
short or long range. That is the nature of it. There are too many

circumstantial changes which a limited being has no control over. He cannot at
all times regulate his mind's entry into or admittance of emotional distresses.
And he cannot always side-step the involuntary motivations which lead to
further distress. Therefore there is no alternative but to perfect the higher yoga
practice of dhyana effortless linkage of his attention to higher concentration
forces and persons. That is the method for getting rid of the psychological
disturbances which cause instability, anxiety and emotional distress.

# Verse 16

heyam dukham anagatam

**heyam- that which is to be avoided; duhkham- distress; anagatam- what has not manifested**

*Distress which is not manifested is to be avoided.*

**Commentary:**

For liberation, a yogin will have to reach a stage where he can sidestep all the merits and demerits which are due to him from providence but which he may sidestep.Both happiness and distress which are coming on the basis of cultural activities from the past are to be avoided at all costs. However a yogin has to advance sufficiently before he can side-step these. It requires insight as to the psychological receptacles which are submissive towards the manifestation of the merits and demerits. A yogin has to close off the opening to such receptacles by practicing kriya yoga.

# Verse 17

### drastr-drsyayoh samyogo heya-hetuh

**drastr-** the observer; **drsyayoh** –of what is perceived; **samyogo-** the indiscriminate association; **heya-** that which is to be avoided; **hetuh-** the cause

*The cause which is to be avoided is the indiscriminate association of the observer and what is perceived.*

## Commentary:

When we identify wholly and solely with what we perceive, we loose objectivity and become attached, rather than detached. This causes a misplaced identity with things which are not in our interest and which make us lose objectivity. Then we experience an impulsive interaction between the new impressions received through the senses and the old impressions stored in the memory (karmasayah). The analytical part of the buddhi organ then hashes over the matter and comes to a conclusion which is shown to us internally in the mind through the magical imagery of the imagination orb. Thus we again come under the spell of the function of that imagination.

If a yogi reaches a stage of control, whereby he stops the impulsive sensual intakes or puts a damper on them as soon as they enter the psyche, he realizes himself as being the perceiver or observer. Then he sees the operations of the senses and the machinations of his memory as being counterproductive. These interact to produce new images which he usually identifies with, to his detriment.

In higher yoga, one is trained in how to distinguish the various parts of the buddhi organ subtle mechanism and the citta mento-emotional energy gyrations. Then one puts an end to the impressions and their varied motivations which destroys one's ability to see beyond the material world.

# Verse 18

prakasa-kriya-sthiti-silam bhutendriyatmakam bhogapavargartham
drsyam

prakasa – clear perception; kriya- action; sthiti- stability; silam- form, disposition; bhuta- mundane elements; indriya- sense organs; atmakam- self, nature; bhoga- experience; apavarga – liberation; artham- value or purpose; drsyam – what is perceived

*What is perceived is of the nature of the mundane elements and the sense organs and is formed in clear perception, action or stability. Its purpose is to give experience or to allow liberation.*

## Commentary:

Whatever we perceive in the subtle or gross mundane energy depends on the condition of the seeing instrument, which is the buddhi organ in the subtle body. According to how it is influenced by and powered by the modes of material nature, it allows either clear perception, impulsive action, or inertia. The purpose behind the interaction of the seer and what is seen, is experience for involvement or experience which results in either bhoga or apavarga.

Material nature has a purpose, either to give more and more varied experiences or pleasurable or harmful experiences or to allow liberation from both. While others hustle after what is pleasurable and try to avoid what might render pain, the yogin strives for liberation by curbing his intellect organ so that he can remain in a clear perception (prakasa).

# Verse 19

visesavisesa-lingamatralingani guna-parvani

visesa- that which is specific; avisesa – what is regular; lingamatra –a mark, that which is indicated; alingani – that which has no indication; guna – influences of material nature; parvani- phases stages parts

*The phases of the influences of material nature are those which are specific, regular, indicated or not indicated.*

## Commentary:

By higher yoga, a yogin gets to see all this clearly: how material nature has certain over-riding phases which it shifts into by its own accord, and which the yogi can enter once he mastered dharana linkage of his attention to higher concentration force, either in or beyond material nature.

The specific objects are those which are perceivable on the gross plane of existence and which are highlighted to our senses because of strong attraction. The non-specific are those gross objects which exhibit mild attraction.

These are regular items like dirt. Even though a gem is a form of dirt, still it is specific. While a speck of mud or a grain of sand are regular, being non-specific. These all have subtle counterparts, which are categorized in the same way and which can be seen through the perception of the subtle body when it is separated from the gross form.

That which is indicated is the subtle matter which we may detect with electronic instruments or discover by mystic techniques in higher yoga. That which has no indication at all is the material energy in it's quiescent stage where it has no differentiation. It is as it were, just nothing at that stage. In higher meditation, one perceives each of these.

# Verse 20

drasta drsimatrah suddho 'pi pratyayanupasyah

drasta – the perceiver; drsi – perception, consciousness; matrah – measure or extent; suddah – purity; api – but; pratyaya- conviction or belief as mental content; anu – following along, patterning after; pasyah – what is perceived

*The perceiver is the pure extent of his consciousness but his conviction is patterned by what is perceived.*

## Commentary:

In actuality the drsi or consciousness which spiritually emanates from the individual self, is itself that self and that self alone. However due to it's absorbent nature, the self loses tract of himself and instead adopts patterns which form in his consciousness as conviction. On the assumption of these convictions one is motivated into cultural activities endlessly.

Sri Patanjali Maharsi used the technical term matra which means a measure of or to an extent. The individual soul is limited. His consciousness radiates only to a certain extent, before it becomes attenuated or is linked to lower or higher concentration forces which help to off-set its limited range.

In the material creation, with a psychic body, the perceiver, the individual self, is itself the pure extent of it's own consciousness. That is its very form. However it functions following along behind what is perceived, thus it is influenced not to realize itself by itself, but to accept itself as its perceptions. These perceptions occur when its pure consciousness is linked to a sending mechanism. The spirit derives a correct or erroneous notion by what he is influenced. By that he transmigrates from one situation to another and is implicated.

# Verse 21

tad-artha eva drsyaya-atma

tad = tat-that; arthah- purpose; eva- only; drsyaya – of what is seen; atma- individual spirit

*The individual spirit who is involved in what is seen exists here for that purpose only.*

### Commentary:

As it is, as we experience it in ourselves, and as we hear from others, this existence is meant for experiencing either ourselves as we are or ourselves as we are connected to various other seeing mechanisms. Basically speaking, a person transmigrates perceiving this or that in the material world. A persons existence here is reduced to that.

# Verse 22

krtartham prati nastam apy anastam tad-anya-sadharanatvat

krt- fulfilled done; artham- purpose; prati – toward; nastam- destroyed, nonexistent, non effective; api – although, but; anastam- not finished, still existing, effective; tat- that; anya- others; sadharanatvat- common, normal, universal

*It is not effective for one to whom its purpose is fulfilled but it has a common effect on the others.*

### Commentary:

The material world loses its effectiveness on a realized yogin. For him its purpose is fulfilled. It no longer operates on him. He no longer reacts to it as others do. For the others however it remains in effect. The others agree on its potency and place stress on it. They accept the convictions derived from it and carry on their social lives.

In a sense this statement of Sri Patanjali is a denial about mass liberation. Here the liberation is individual and only for those who have retracted their spiritual energy from linkage into the subtle mundane sensing energy.

Others will remain in the material world, because its effects hold them here, utilizing their attention.

Sri Krishna in the Bhagavad-Gita did not profess any mass liberation of many living entities, neither by an act of faith nor by belief or confidence. He too singled out individual yogis for liberation. This is what he said:

*manusyanam sahasresu*

*kascid yatati siddhaye*

*yatatam api siddhanam*

*kascin mam vetti tattvatah*

**Someone, in thousands of human beings, strives for psychological perfection. Of those who endeavor, even of those who are perfected, someone knows Me in truth. (Gita 7.3)**

# Verse 23

sva-svami-saktyoh svarupa-upalabdhi-hetuh samyogah

sva – own nature, own psyche; swami- the master, the individual self; saktyoh – of the potency of the two; svarupa- own form; upalabdhi- obtaining experience; hetuh – cause, reason; samyoga-conjunction

*There is a reason for the conjunction of the individual self and his psychological energies. It is for obtaining the experience of his own form.*

## Commentary:

This states indirectly that the living entity who has a psychological make-up can only realize his essential or spiritual nature, by first coming in contact with the subtle material nature and then differentiating himself from that mundane power.

The conjunction (samyoga) is enforced, because no limited being has the power to join himself with material nature nor to disconnect himself with it. This is why Sri Patanjali acknowledged that special person who taught even the ancient yogis.

*klesa karma vipaka 'sayair aparam-rstah purusa visesa isvarah*

**The Supreme Lord is that special person who is not affected by troubles, actions, development or by subconsciousmotivations. (Yoga Sutra 1:24)**

*tatra niratisayam sarvajna bijam*

**There, in Him, is found the unsurpassed origin of all knowledge. (Yoga Sutra 1:25)**

*purvesam api guruh kalena navacchedat*

**He, that that this particular person, being unconditioned by time is the guru even of the ancient teachers, the authorities from before. (Yoga Sutra 1:26)**

*tasya vacakah pranavah*

**Of Him, the sacred syllable Aum (Om) is the designation. (Yoga Sutra 1:27)**

The ultimate purpose of the conjunction is for the limited beings to objectively realize their spiritual selves, apart from and distinct from the subtle material nature which they accept initially as their personal psychology.

The individual self is supposed to be the master, the swami of his psychological powers but initially he is overtaken, influenced and dominated by them. Thus he has the task of realizing what happened to his autonomy.

# Verse 24

**tasya hetur avidya**

**tasya – of it; hetuh – cause; avidya – spiritual ignorance**

*The cause of the conjunction is spiritual ignorance.*

### Commentary:

Besides the fact that there is a forced conjunction between the individual limited spirits and the mundane sensing energies, there is also an underlying reason for this, which is innate spiritual ignorance of the limited beings. They did not understand themselves to be begin with. The Supreme Being may be blamed for putting the limited beings in peril by forcing them into conjunction with the mundane psychology, but the reason for His action is stated in this verse; being the spiritual ignorance of these limited dependents of His.

As far as the Supreme Being was concerned, the only way to free us from that ignorance was to put us in conjunction with the mundane psychology. From that position we may derive disgust (nirvedah) with that energy and then through introspection study ourselves and our linkage with it and with His assistance, work for emancipation.

The blame placed on the Supreme Being is lifted from Him as soon as we understand we were with an innate and primeval spiritual ignorance of our true nature. The contrast between ourselves and the mundane energy is the only aspect that motivates us to realize ourselves.

# Verse 25

tad-abhavat samyoga abhavo hanam tad drseh kaivalyam

tad= tat- that spiritual ignorance; abhavat- resulting from the elimination; samyoga – conjunction;  abhavah – disappearance, elimination; hanam – withdrawal, escape; tad = tat- that; drseh- of the perceiver; kaivalyah- total separation from the mundane psychology

*The elimination of the conjunction which results from the elimination of that spiritual ignorance is the withdrawal that is the total separation of the perceiver from the mundane psychology.*

## Commentary:

Yogis should take care in studying this verse, to get Sri Patanjali's definition of kaivalyam. This term has come down to us as meaning various forms of liberation, all depending on the spiritual sect which advocated it. However, to understand Sri Patanjali, we must stick to his definitions. Clearly, kaivalya is defined in this verse, within the context of what Sri Patanjali spoke of, which is the samyoga or conjunction between the individual spirit and his subtle mundane psychology (sva). This psychology is hinted at in the second verse of chapter one, as operational vrittis:

*yogas citta vrtti nirodhah*

**"The skill of yoga demonstrated by the conscious non-operation of the vibrational modes of the mento-emotional energy."(Yoga Sutra 1:2)**

There is no definition here of kaivalyam being union with God or oneness with God or anything like that. It does not mean here that one has become God or that one has merged into the Absolute Truth. Sri Patanjali in the context, spoke of the complete isolation of the individual limited spirit from his psychological sensing mechanisms which are derived from material nature and his situating himself and realizing himself as his own spiritual nature in its purity by restricting himself to it and to its pure extent.

*drasta drsimatrah suddho `pi pratyaya ‘nupasyah*

"The perceiver is the pure extent of his consciousness but his conviction is patterned by what is perceived."(Yoga Sutra 2:20)

# Verse 26

**viveka-khyatir aviplava hanopayah**

**viveka – discrimination; khyatih – insight; aviplava – unbroken, continuous; hanopaya = hana - avoidance + upayah – means, method**

*The method for avoiding that spiritual ignorance is the establishment of continuous discriminative insight.*

## Commentary:

Vivekakathyatih is discriminative insight, gained through higher yoga practice or naturally occurring as a result of actively using a yoga siddha form or a spiritual body. It is not book knowledge nor concepts derived from authorative teachers. Most person will have to do yoga to develop this, even though a rare few might have this naturally occurring in their yoga siddha or spiritual forms.

Spiritual ignorance (avidya) which is the ignorance of the difference between one's spiritual energy and its linkage or mixture with mundane psychology, is removed by no other method besides the development of the discriminative insight.

# Verse 27

tasya saptadha pranta-bhumih prajna

**tasya** – of his, khyati vivekakhyati – discriminative insight; **saptadha** – seven fold; **pranta**- boundary or edge +**bhumih** –territory, range; **prantabhumih** – stage; **prajna** – insight

*Concerning the development of his discriminative insight, there are seven stages.*

### Commentary:

Sri Patanjali clarified that in developing the discriminative insight, one moves through seven stages. It does not come overnight. One develops it step by step.

# Verse 28

yoga-anga-anusthanad asuddhi-ksye jnana-diptir a viveka-khyateh

yoganganusthanat = yoga- yoga process + anga-part + anusthanat-from consistent practice; asuddhih – impurities; ksaye – on the elimination; jnanadiptih- radiant organ of perception; avivekakhyateh = a- till, until, up to + viveka- discrimination + khyateh – insight

*From the consistent practice of the parts of the yoga process, on the elimination of the impurity, the radiant organ of perception becomes manifest, until there is steady discriminative insight.*

## Commentary:

There is really no short cut, except to practice steadily and persistently with attention from day to day. From that, the impurities gradually diminish, until they fade altogether. Then the organ of perception, the buddhi organ in the subtle body, becomes radiant. It emits a light and sees super-naturally and spiritually. This is the jnana dipah or jnanadiptih. It is also called jnanachakshuh. When there is consistent practice in using this vision in dhyana and Samadhi yoga, then there is steady consistent discriminative insight for the yogi, not otherwise.

# Verse 29

yama-niyama-asana-pranayama-pratyhara-dharana-dhyana-
samadhayo'stav-angani

yama- moral restrains; niyama – recommended behaviors; asana-
body postures; pranayama- breath enrichment of the subtle body;
pratyahar- sensual energy withdrawal; dharana- linking of the attention
to higher concentration forces or persons; dhyana- effortless linkage of
the attention to higher concentration forces or persons; samdhayah-
continuous effortless linkage of the attention to higher concentration
forces or persons; astau- eight; angani- parts of a thing

*Moral restrains, recommended behaviors, body posture, breath
enrichment, sensual energy withdrawal, linking of the attention to higher
concentration forces or persons, effortless linkage of the attention to
higher concentration forces or persons, continuous linkage of the attention
to higher concentration forces or persons are the eight parts of the yoga
system.*

## Commentary:

Sri Goraksnath in his writings gave six parts to yoga, leaving out the preliminary
parts of yama, moral restraints and niyama, recommended behaviors. This
is because those two are very preliminary. A person who has not integrated
those, must instill them in himself as he practices the other more advanced
portions.I experienced many students who are not masterful at the preliminary
stages. They should master these as they proceed and find that their lack of
skill in cultural dealings causes impediments. According to the advisories and
warnings issued by Sri Krishna to Arjuna in the Bhagavad-gita, a person who
does not have an exemption from cultural activities, cannot succeed fully in
yoga. Actually the sooner that a yogi can realize this, the better and more
advanced he will be. If he does not cooperate with the central person in the
Universal Form, with Sri Krishna, he will not be able to get to the Samadhi
stage. It will be impossible.

Sri Gorakashnath did not want the Hatha yogis, his students, to waste their
time and energy in the moral field, in trying to perfect righteous living, but
nevertheless, if one does not work his way cautiously through the cultural
world, one will fail at yoga practice. We must understand that Sri Gorakshnath
is a birth taken by Sri Skanda Kumara, the celibate son of Lord Shiva. As such
he never advocates grhasta ashram but that does not mean that is has no value.
We have to understand its value, just in case we require another human form.
The moral restraints and recommended behaviors have their usage to keep
us on the good side of King Dharma, the supernatural person who sponsors
righteous life style.

# Verse 30

**ahimsa-satya-asteya-brahmacarya-aparigraha yamah**

**ahimsa - non violence ; satya- realism ; asteya - non stealing; brahmacarya = sexual non-expressiveness which results in the perception of spirituality; aparigrahah= non – possessiveness; yamah- moral restraints**

*Non-violence, realism, non-stealing, sexual non-expressiveness which results in the perception of spirituality (Brahman) and non-possessiveness are the moral restraints.*

## Commentary:

Some authorities list other moral restraints, but these given by Sri Patanjali cover the entire listing of the negative qualities which are to be avoided. This is the list of qualities which should be cultivated if they are not innate to one's character.

Ahimsa is the attitude of genuine harmlessness towards other creatures, not just human beings. Of course a yogi has to know that the human form of life is comparatively more valuable than other species, but he should know as well that creatures who are in other life forms must fulfill their gratifications there before they could be permanently transformed to higher forms. Their lives should not be under-rated. A yogi should not assume a master-of-the-species attitude. He should not harm any other creature willfully. He should situate himself circumstantially so that occasions for killing do not arise.

According to Lord Mahavira and other Tirthankaras in the Jain disciplic succession, we have no business killing other creatures. A yogin should be non-violent. If one finds that he has a violent nature or that a part of his psyche takes pleasure in harming others or in seeing others being hurt, then he should work to purify that part. Each yogin has to realize defects and work to remove them by the relevant yoga kriyas.

Satya or realism includes truthfulness, but for the yogin it is more than conventional honesty. It has to do with developing the deep insight described by Sri Patanjali in the previous verse as jnana-diptih and as vivekakhyatih. This gives one deep insight into reality, even to perceive past lives and to properly interpret the samskara subconscious impressions which are buried deep in memory and which surface from time to time.

Asteya or non-stealing is a must for a yogin. The tendency for stealing is innate in the subtle body. A yogin has to work with himself to eliminate it. This requires vigilance.

Brahmacarya has a conventional meaning as celibacy but it is more than that. It is an active or dynamic celibacy which is assisted by yoga practice and which results in the perception of Brahman or spiritual reality. This means mastership of celibacy yoga, so that even in an adult body, the sexual urge is sublimated and does not arise to disturb the psyche. A celibate yogi should not have sexual intercourse unless he or she desires to have a child. He should ideally only have as many intercourses as there are children produced from his or her body. This is the ideal behavior. Failing in this a yogin has to work with his psyche to improve its sexual outlook, so that eventually its sexual needs are eliminated by the practice of celibacy yoga and kundalini yoga. Without attaining celibacy one cannot become liberated. It is not possible, because the energy of the subtle body will not be efficiently used if sexual expression continues through it. Thus one will not realize the subtle mundane existence which is preliminary for spiritual seekers.

Aaparigrahah or non-possessiveness has to do with understanding that whatever we encounter in the gross or subtle existence is the property of more powerful beings. The only real possession we have is the task of our purification. The critical nature within us which usually seeks external expression should be directed backward into the psyche. This redirected critical force improves our condition by the application of corrective tendencies.

Overall these moral restraints are necessary for a yogi, but he does not master these initially , even though this is listed as the first stage of yoga. He masters this a little and then he continues to get more control of his nature as he advances and sees more and more how subtle the defects are and how mystic and specific he must be to root them out.

# Verse 31

jati-desa-kala-samaya-anavacchinnah sarva-bhauma maha-vratam

jati–status; desa–location; kala–time; samya-condition; anavacchinnah-not restricted by, not adjusted by; sarvabhaumah- relating to all standard stages, being standard; mahavratam- great commitment

*Those moral restraints are not to be adjusted by the status, location, time and condition, they are related to all stages of yoga, being the great commitment.*

## Commentary:

Sarvabhauma means relating to all the earth. However bhauma, as a synonym, also means stage or foreground, as explained in verse 27 with the term prantabhumih. In all the stages of yoga, the first stages maintain relevance. Thus the yogi never reaches a stage where he can completely ignore moral restraints, except when he is released from the material world completely.

Sri Patanjali accredited those moral restraints as the great commitment (mahavrata).

# Verse 32

sauca-samtosa-tapah-svadhyaya-isvara-pranidhanani niyamah

sauca- purification; santosa- contentment; tapah- austerity; svadhyaya – study of the psyche; isvara- Supreme Lord; pranidhanani- profound religious meditation; niyamah- recommended behaviors

*Purification, contentment, austerity and profound religious meditation on the Supreme Lord are the recommended behaviors.*

## Commentary:

Many religious leaders ridicule Sri Patanjali because he classified profound religious meditation to the Supreme Lord as part of an elementary stage in yoga practice, but just as the first stage remains relevant throughout the practices (sarva-bhaumah verse 31), so also every other stage remains in place, and is improved upon as the yogi moves to higher levels.

According to some critics, Sri Patanjali hawked too much about yoga and neglected the bhakti or bhakti-yoga, giving it an insignificant place in the layout of spiritual disciplines. However if one checks the Bhagavad-Gita carefully, he will discover that Sri Krishna, who declared Himself as the Supreme Lord, gave high precedence to yoga.

The other aspect of Sri Patanjali's treatment of devotion to God, is understood when we consider the term pranidhanani. Sri Patanjali spoke of profound religious meditation. This is a mystic process of internal focus upon the Supreme Lord, to reach the Divinity in a totally different dimension. But why one may ask did Sri Patanjali not place this as the foremost aspect of yoga practice? The reason is simple: One cannot do this unless one first masters yoga. The skill to do this comes only by perfecting the yoga austerities.

**In the Bhagavad-Gita, the purpose of yoga is defined by Sri Krishna in the following terms:**

*tatrai'kagram manah krtva*

*yatacittendriyakriyah*

*upavisya'sane yunjyad*

*yogam atmavisuddhaye*

…being there, seated in a posture, having the mind focused, the person who controls his thinking and sensual energy, should practice the yoga discipline for self-purification. (Gita 6:12)

**Sri Krishna also explained that a yogi should commit himself to cultural activities for the sake of psychic purification:**

*kayena manasa buddhya*

*kevalair indriyair api*

*yoginah karma kurvanti*

*sangam tyaktva'tmasuddhaye*

With the body, mind and intelligence, or even with the senses alone, the yogis, having discarded attachment, perform cultural acts for self-purification. (Gita 5:11)

**Sri Patanjali does not contradict Sri Krishna. In fact he reinforces what Sri Krishna said.**

# Verse 33

**vitarka-badhane pratipaksa-bhavanam**

vitarka- doubt, argument; bandhane- in annoyance or disturbance; pratipaksa – what is opposite or contrary; bhavanam- manifesting, imagining, conceiving, considering

*In the case of the annoyance produced by doubts, one should conceive of what is opposite.*

## Commentary:

When there are any doubts regarding the moral restraints and the recommended behavior, a yogi should counteract that state of mind by conceiving of the opposite. In other words, sometimes a yogi is pressured by the same status, location, time or condition mentioned in verse 31. Then he may cast aside the five great commitments, feeling that he is allowed to do so because of a particular status he is awarded by providence, or because of a location which he is in, or through the time of an occurrence, or because he was pressured by certain conditions. However Sri Patanjali objects and states that the yogi should not give in but should hold to the principles by considering and contemplating the opposite type of actions which correspond with the five great commitments.

If a yogi remembers this instruction his course into higher yoga would be accelerated, otherwise he will be stalled in lower stages for a very long time. Sometimes a yogi gets an idea to do something which jeopardizes his practice. He may feel that he must do it to comply with a pressure of providence which is forced into his mind. Usually, such a situation will pass on even if the yogi does not satisfy the urges, but if he is rash, he will act in the wrong way and forestall his practice. Thus Sri Patanjali ask that there be considerations to the contrary, anytime we get some idea to do something that is against the moral principles.

Sometimes in the astral world and in parallel dimensions a yogi is circumstantially positioned for breaking moral rules, but when he gets back into this material body and recalls the incident, he regrets it or he thinks that for some reason he was unable to use his discrimination.Sri Patanjali mentioned this discriminative insight before under the terms of vivekakhyatih. Unless this is developed to the extent that it is carried everywhere the yogi may go through this and into other dimensions, he will of necessity break the moral restraints here or there, whenever his discriminative insight vanishes or is weakened.

# Verse 34

vitarka himsadayah krta-karita-anumodita lobha-krodha-moha-purvaka mrdu-madhya-adhimatra dukha-ajnana-ananta-phala iti pratipaksa-bhavanam

vitarkah- doubts; himsa- violence; adayah- and related matters; krta – done; karita – cause to be done; anumoditah- endorsed, approved; lobha- greed; krodha- anger; moha- delusion; purvakah- caused by, proceeded by; mrdu – minor; madhya- mediocre; adhimatrah- substantial; duhkha – distress; ajnana – spiritual ignorance; ananta- endless; phalah- results; iti – thus; pratipaksa – opposite type; bhavanam – considerations

*Doubts which produce violence and related actions, which are performed, caused to be done or endorsed, and which are caused by greed, anger and delusion, even if minor, mediocre or substantial, cause endless distress and spiritual ignorance as the results. Therefore, one should consider the opposite features.*

## Commentary:

Violence and related actions are those which run contrary to the moral restraints of non-violence, realism, non-stealing, sexual non-expressiveness and non-possessiveness. Any ideas which run contrary to morality and which seem to justify such immoral acts are to be abandoned. If a yogin finds that he does not have the power to abandon immoral acts, then he should deeply think of the benefit of morality. This may give him the required detachment and invoke in him sufficient patience so that he restrains from the vices until the impulsions pass out of his mind or loose their impulsive force.

If a moral code is to be broken at a certain time, it will be done by someone somehow because if the energy or motivation for that act, finds the yogi to be an unwilling subject, it will move away from him and influence some other person to act. A yogi should understand this. A yogi may be tricked again and again by those compulsions to do immoral acts but then after a time, he will begin to develop a resistance to those forceful motivations, which cause him to deviate. Sri Arjuna questioned Sri Krishna about this in the Bhagavad-gita:

*arjuna uvaca*

*atha kena prayukto'yam*

*papam carati purusah*

*anicchann api varsneya*

*balad iva niyojitah*

Arjuna said: Then explain, O family man of the Vrsnis, by what is a person forced to commit an evil even unwillingly, just as if he were compelled to do so? (Gita 3.36)

# Verse 35

**ahimsa-pratisthayam tat-sannidhau vaira-tyagah**

ahimsa = non – violence; pratisthayam – on being firmly established; tat- his; sannidhau – presence, vicinity; vaira – hostility; tyagah – abandonment

*On being firmly estsablished in non-violence, the abandonment of hostility occurs in his presence.*

### Commentary:

This charm over the violent nature of others, is sometimes exhibited by great yogins. Sometimes haphazardly it is manifested in the life of student yogins. It begins in human society where people who are normally hostile to each other exhibit undue kindness even to their enemies, when they are in a presence of a yogin.

The force of the non-violent nature of the yogi disarms and temporarily disintegrates the hostile nature of others. Sometimes this is shown when a fish-eating human being is in the presence of a great yogin. The fish-eater feels as if he cannot eat fish but must eat vegetarian or fruitarian meals. But that violent nature is again manifested when the person gets out of the range of the yogin. On the contrary however, sometimes it is seen that a great yogin has no effect on a cannibal, or flesh-eater. This is because the lower tendencies may be so strong as to resist saintly influence or it may be that the yogin assumes a sensual withdrawal attitude, intending not to adjust the evolutionary development of others.

# Verse 36

satya-pratisthayam kriya-phalasrayatvam

**satya** – realism; **pratisthayam**- on being established; **kriya**- actions; **phala**- results; **asryatvam**- what serves as a support for something else

*On being established in realism, his actions serve as a basis for results.*

## Commentary:

It may be contested that in all cases, a person's action serve as the basis of the results he will be afforded by providence, either for good or bad, according to what was committed . However the yogi is more conscious of his actions and their potential results than others. This is because of mystic perception in the truths of how this world operates. Thus a yogi's actions, particularly his mystic actions do confirm with reality and are consistent with realism.

In these verses instead of using the term tishta, Sri Patanjali uses pratishtha which means to be firmly established, not just to be initially or haphazardly established. This comes after sufficient practice or in the case of the divine beings, it is from their superior nature.

# Verse 37

**asteya-pratisthayam sarva-ratnopasthanam**

asteya= non-stealing; pratisthayam- on firmly establishing; sarva- all; ratna- gems, precious things; upasthanam- approaching, waiting upon

*On being firmly established in non-sealing, all precious things wait to serve a yogin.*

## Commentary:

Still, usually a yogin is not concerned about these things. This is because his mind is fixed on the most precious thing with is his yoga practice. Thus many opportunities for exploitation come to a yogin but he does not take advantage of them. People often wonder why a great yogi wastes his life away, and why he does not exploit all the people and resources which are in a position to be used by him. The answer is that a yogi is too preoccupied with yoga practice. A great yogin is easily discovered if one searches for the person around whom, all sorts of wealth manifest but who does not use any of that wealth and who is indifferent to it, seemingly stupid, seemingly not realizing the worth in valuables and in the cheap labor which could be derived from others.

# Verse 38

**brahmacarya-pratishayam virya-labah**

**brahmacarya - sexual non-expressiveness which results in the perception of spirituality; pratisthayam- being firmly established; virya- vigor; labhah- what is gained**

*On being firmly established in the sexual non-expressiveness which results in the perception of spirituality, vigor is gained.*

### Commentary:

This means dynamic celibacy established by virtue of yoga practice in terms of asana postures and pranayama breath nutrition methods which will be mentioned forthwith by Sri. Patanjali.

This is the urdhvareta stage where the yogi masters kundalini yoga and celibacy yoga.

# Verse 39

aparigraha-sthairye janma-kathamta-sambodhah

**aparigraha** - non-possessiveness; **sthairaya**- in the consistent; **janma**-birth; **kathamta**- how, the reason for; **sambodhah**- full or correct perception regarding something

*In being consistent in non possessiveness, there is manifested the reason and the correct perception regarding one's birth.*

### Commentary:

When a yogi has mastered the quality of non-possessiveness in relation to this gross level of reality, his energy of appreciation shifts to the subtle reality. Thus he perceives the reason for the births he recently took. If he develops that clairvoyant skill, he comes to understand why others took up a certain body. He can know his past lives and that of others. However, if realizing that he has this skill, he becomes attracted to popularity and wants to be endearing and beloved, he might abuse himself. Thus, the skill will gradually leave him as he becomes more and more in the habit of appropriating fame in the material world.

# Verse 40

saucha svanga-jugupsa parair asamsargah

saucat- from purification; svanga= sva-oneself+ anga- limbs; jugupsa – aversion, disgust; parair = pariah – with others; asamsargah = non-association, lack of desire to associate

*From purification comes a disgust for one's own body and a lack of desire to associate with others.*

### Commentary:

True purification comes after long and hard yoga austerities. Thus the student yogi once he has earned purity of his psyche, develops a disgust for the same material body through which he worked hard to develop that purity. This is because the material body and the subtle one which caused it, has an innate tendency to absorb the pollutions which pull an ascetic down from yoga practice. As soon as a student yogi stops practice, he regresses. Even though the material body is an asset, still it always remains as a liability so long as it exists. Worse, still, is the lower subtle body, because until one can shed it off and take on a yoga siddha form, one is in danger of being degraded. The lower subtle body is worse than the gross form when it comes to adaptation and acceptance of vices.

A yogi develops a lack of desire to associate with others, except for his advanced teachers. This is because in such association he or she always runs the risks of degradation, due to susceptibility to the habits of others. People think that a yogi hates them or avoids them. Actually a yogi has no time to hate anyone because he has to attend to his practice and the energy which would be used to hate others is needed to accelerate the progress. But he develops a desire not to associate with others. This happens as a matter of course. It is a result of higher yoga practice.

# Verse 41

sattvasuddhi-saumanasyaikagryendriya-jayatma-darsana-yogyatvani ca

sattva – being, nature, psyche; suddhi – purification; saumanasya – concerning benevolence; ekagra- ability to link the attention to one concentration force or person; indriya- sensual energy; jaya – conquest; atma – spirit; darsana- sight, vision; yogyatvani – being fit for yoga or abstract meditation; ca- and

*Purification of the psyche results in benevolence, the ability to link the attention to one concentration force or person, conquest of the sensual energy, vision of the spirit and fitness for abstract meditation.*

### Commentary:

Purification of the psyche (sattva-suddhi) is possible only after celibacy yoga is mastered. Then the student yogi develops benevolence towards everyone. This is a type of detachment but in its social application it functions as benevolence or good will towards one and all.

This student yogi develops the ability to link his mind to one concentration force in the dharana sixth stage of yoga practice. He masters the sensual energy by perfecting the pratyahar fifth stage, and is able to begin the dhyana seventh stage, to have the vision of the spirit and a fitness for abstract meditation. This is not impersonal meditation as some profess, but it is rather meditation on levels above this physical world and above the lower astral regions.

# Verse 42

santosad anuttamah sukha-labhah

santosat- from contentment; anuttamah – supreme, the very best; sukha – happiness; labhah – obtained

*From contentment, the very best in happiness is obtained.*

## Commentary:

This is a calm type of happiness devoid of the excitations which come from the pursuit of cravings and vices. A yogi appreciates this contentment which others dislike because it lacks excitement.

# Verse 43

**kayendriya-siddhir asuddhi-ksayat tapasah**

**kaya – body; indriya- sensual energy; siddhih- skill, perfection; asuddhi-impurity; ksayat- from the elimination; tapasah- austerity**

*Austerity, resulting in the elimination of impurity produces perfection of the body and sensual energy.*

## Commentary:

This is the basic of result gained in the gruesome austerities of asana and pranayam, the third and fourth stages of yoga practice. When the impurities in the subtle body are removed, one gains a skill in controlling the gross and subtle bodies as well as the sensual energy which is housed in them. This is mastered in Kundalini yoga, celibacy yoga and purity-of-the-psyche yoga (sattvasuddhi (verse 41), (atmasuddha bhg. 6:12).

Tapasah means austerity. One may ask which austerity? This question is answered in the term asuddhiksayat, which means the austerities which result in the elimination of ksayat or impurities.

# Verse 44

swadhyaya ista-devata-samprayogah

**svadhyayat- from study of the psyche; istadevata – cherished divine being; samprayogah- intimate contact**

*From study of the psyche, comes intimate contact with the cherished divine being.*

### Commentary:

Sri Patanjali has not named the istadevata, the cherished divine personality, who the student yogi aspires to be with. However for the yogi, that person might be different than He is for some other ascetic. There are many of these divine beings who serve as cherished Lords of the limited entities.

However, when the yogi has achieved complete purity of the psyche, he gets a divine vision through which he meets the cherished deity face to face and can relate with that Personality of Godhead.

# Verse 45

samadhisiddhih isvarapranidhanat

samadhi – continuous effortless linkage of the attention to a highter concentration force or person; siddhih – perfection, skill; isvara – supreme lord; pranidhanat – from the profound religious meditation

*From the profound religious meditation upon the Supreme Lord comes the perfection of continuous effortless linkage of the attention to that Divinity.*

## Commentary:

Now all accusations upon Sri Patanjali regarding his alleged ideas of impersonalism and atheism are totally denied. Sri Patanjali Maharshi was undoubtedly a theist of the first order. Sri B.K. S. Iyengar in his translation and commentary on the sutras explained that Patanjali was an incarnation of Lord Adishesha, the divine serpentine bedstead of Lord Vishnu. Patanjali's mother was named Gonika.

# Verse 46

sthira-sukham asanam

sthira – steady; sukham – comfortable; asanan – bodily posture

*The posture should be steady and comfortable.*

### Commentary:

The yoga asana for meditation should one that is steady and comfortable. Ideally, one should sit for meditation in the lotus posture, the padmasana, if that posture is unsteady and uncomfortable, one should practice to improve it. During meditation one should use a posture that keeps the body steady and mind at ease. As one practices more and more, the difficult postures become easier and easier to perform.

# Verse 47

prayatna-saithilyananta-samapattibhyam

**prayatna – effort; saithilya – relaxation; ananta- endless, infinite; samapattibhyam – meeting, encounter**

*It results in relaxation of effort and the meeting with the infinite.*

## Commentary:

Asana is perfected when it becomes steady and comfortable, so much so that the yogin relaxes his efforts to hold the body in the posture. He shifts his attention to link it with the infinite.

# Verse 48

tato dvandvanabhighatah

tatah – then; dvandvah - the dualities of happiness and distress, heat and cold; anabhighatah – not shrinking, no attacking, not botheration

*From then on, there are no botherations from the dualities like happiness and distress, heat and cold.*

## Commentary:

When there is perfect posture of body in which the yogin attains continuous effortless linkage of his attention to a higher concentration force, or divine person, then the botheration of the mento-emotional energy which concerns happiness and distress cease for him. These continue in the life of the student yogins who are on a lower level of practice. They should master themselves through a more consistent practice.

# Verse 49

tasmin sati svasa-prasvasayor gati-vicchedah pranayamah

tasmin – on this; sati – being accomplished; svasa- inhalation; prasvasayoh – of the exhalation; gati – the flow; vicchedah –the separation; pranayama – breath regulation

*Once this is accomplished, breath regulation, which is the seperation of the flow of inhalation and exhalation, is attained.*

## Commentary:

The pranayama cannot be mastered properly until one has mastered postures or asanas but that does not mean that preliminary pranayama cannot be learned before hand. All the stages of yoga are learned one by one or even haphazardly according to one's destiny regarding availability of knowledgeable teachers. One cannot focus properly on the vital force until one has mastered a suitable posture. This is the point but one can become familiar with the various pranayamas before hand.

A yogin has to learn how to separate the flow of the breath, so that the inhalation is distinct from the exhalation, so that there is a pause between these. This is why the word *vicchedah* was used. It means separation, cleavage, or gap. Generally, mammals breath in and out without pause because their breath is not complete or sufficient. It is usually shallow. The out breath is rushed in to speed up the next intake of air. When one reconditions his lung apparatus, so that the intake is complete, this rush for exhalations in order to inhale again, ceases. And the separation of the intake and out breath becomes evident, along with the benefits of that for meditation.

# Verse 50

**bahyabhyantara-stambha-vrttir desakala-samkhyabhih paridrsto dirgha-suksmah**

bahya – external; abhyantara- internal; stambha- restrained, suppressed, restrictive; vrttih- activity, movement operation; desa – place; kala- time; samkhyabhih – with numbering accounting; paridrstah- measured, regulated; dirgha – prolonged; suksmah – subtle, hardly noticeable

*It has internal, external and restrictive operations, which are regulated according to the place, time and accounting, being prolonged or hardly noticeable.*

### Commentary:

Ideally, pranayama is learned from a teacher who practiced to proficiency. Such teachers are hard to find. The first accomplishment of a student yogi is to learn how to fill the nadis in the subtle form. When that is achieved, he will discover other pranayamas automatically by the grace of the force of prana and by the awakening of the kundalini chakra.

Pranayama teachers usually stress a count for alternate breathing in the ration of 1:4:2, meaning that one should inhale through one nostril for one count, then retain the air for four counts and then exhale all air through the other nostril during two counts, such that if one starts inhaling through the right nostril alone, one will hold the air, then expel it through the left nostril. Then begin the cycle by inhaling through the left nostril, holding and expelling the air through the right nostril. Eventually one should increase the duration, so that the time for a count increase. This is done without straining the lung system. If the nadies are not fully charged before one begins, and if one is not a celibate yogi, one will not be successful with this practice. There are many preliminary practices required for success in yoga. One would be fortunate if he or she could learn these from an accomplished teacher.

# Verse 51

**bahy-abhyantara-visaya-aksepi caturthah**

**bahya – external; abhyantara – internal; visaya – objective; aksepi – transcending; caturthah – the fourth**

*That which transcends the objective external and internal breath regulation is the fourth type of pranayama.*

## Commentary:

In the previous sutra, Sri Patanjali listed three types of operations, relating to internal, external and restrictive operations of the breath. Then he gave a fourth operating having to do with transcending the objective of the preliminary three operations.

# Verse 52

tatah ksiyate prakasa-avaranam

**tatah – thence, from that; ksiyate – is dissipated; prakasa – light; avaranam – covering, mental darkness**

*From that is dissipated, the mental darkness which veils the light.*

## Commentary:

The advanced pranayama is done after much practice. It's mastership does not come easy. The result of it, is clear to a yogi because the dark mind space is cleared off and a brilliant light is perceived. This light is illuminating (prakasa).

# Verse 53

dharanasu ca yogyata manasah

**dharanasu-** for linking the attention to a higher concentration force or person; **ca** – and; **yogyata-** being conducive for abstract meditation; **manasah-** of the mind

> *. . . and the state of the mind for linking the attention to a higher concentration force or person.*

## Commentary:

Dharana practice requires a preliminary mastership in certain aspects of prana energy control. This is why when someone sits to meditate without first doing pranayama , he cannot be successful even though he may imagine for himself in peace happiness and light. One has to make the mind fit for yoga practice (yogyata manasah). The mind will prevent the attention from linking to a higher concentration force or person if the mind itself is not surcharged with a higher grade of pranic energy. It will be unable to make a higher linkage, except now and again, by a fluke, haphazardly. For consistent practice one must do the asana with pranayama daily before meditation practice.

# Verse 54

sva-visaya-asamprayoge cittasya-svarupa-anukara ivendriyanam
pratyaharah

sva –their own; visaya – objects of perception; asamprayoge – in not
contacting; cittasya- of the mento-emotional energy; svarapa –own
form; anukarah – imitation, patterning, assuming; iva – as if, as it were;
indriyanam – senses; pratyaharah – withdrawal of sensual energy and its
focus on the mind

*The withdrawal of the senses, is as it were, their assumption of the form
of mento- emotional energy when not contacting their own objects of
perception.*

## Commentary:

In his word for word meanings, Sri B.K.S. Iyengar gave as the root word for
pratyaharah. He gave the basic parts of that Sanskrit word as follows:

prati+ang+hr meaning to draw towards the opposite.

When the mento-emotional energy, the citta, is outward bound, it is called
sensual energy or indriyani. But when it is inward bound it is called citta or
emotional force. A yogin has to master that citta energy and reorient it so that
it gives up it's outward bound habit.

# Verse 55

tatah parama vasyatendriyanam

tatah – then, from that accomplishment; parama – highest, greatest; vasyata – subdued, subjugation, control; indriyanam - of the sense

*From that accomplishment, comes the highest degree of control of the senses.*

### Commentary:

Pratyahar practice when mastered, gives the student yogin, the qualification to practice higher yoga, which are mainly actions on the mystic plane.

# 3
# Vibhūti-pāda
# (Mystic Powers)

The third chapter finishes the descriptions of the balance of the eight limbs of yoga and presents information on samyama and the attainment of certain paranormal powers.

# Verse 1

**desha-bandhash chittasya dharana**

**desa- location ; bandhah- confinement, restriction ; cittasya- of the mento-emotional energy; dharana- linking of the attention to a concentration force or person**

*Linking of the attention to a concentration force or person, involves a restricted location in the mento-emotional energy.*

## Commentary:

For higher meditation, everything is within the mental and emotional energy fields. This is the psychological environment from which a yogin can break out of this dimension to enter other parallel worlds which are either subtle, supernatural or spiritual. It is from within the mento-emotional energy that one breaks out of this world. The paradox of it is this: the very same mental and emotional energy which caused us to become attached to this world, can also in turn, cause liberation. The gate for exiting this world is in the same mento-emotional energy (cittasya).

Many people feel that a yogi enters into his own psyche, develops it, feels powerful as God and then becomes perfect. Little do they understand that from within his own psyche a yogi finds entry into parallel worlds. From particular locations, desa, particular limiting or confining locations (desa bandhah), a yogi finds doorways and peep holes that give him access to other worlds, places that he might be transferred after permanently leaving his physical body.

# Verse 2

### tatra pratyayaikatanata dhyanam

atra- there, in that location; prtyaya- conviction or belief as mental content, instinctive interest; ekatanata- one continuous threadlike flow of attention = eka-one = tana- thread of fiber; dhyananam- effortless linking of the attention to a higher concentration force or person

*When in that location, there is one continuous threadlike flow of ones instinctive interest that is the effortless linking of the attention to a higher concentration force or person.*

### Commentary:

The key term in this verse is pratayaya. Shivram Apte in his Sanskrit English Dictionary gave the following meanings: conviction, settled belief, trust, faith, conception, idea, and notion. I have given instinctive interest as the meaning. In any case, when that (pratayaya) flows in a continuous threadlike motion at th place of focus, then it is the dhyana, seventh stage of yoga practice.

The Raj Yogi I.I. Taimni gave stretching or streaming unbrokenly as one, as the meaning for ekatanata. student yogi would do well for himself by carefully studying the Sanskrit of this verse, because it is no sufficient to say that dharana is concentration, dhyana is contemplation or meditation as we are accustomed to. Such definitions are too vague.

# Verse 3

tad evarthamatra-nirbhasam varupa-shunyam iva samadhih

tadeva= tat-that + eva – only, alone; artha- purpose objective; matra – only, merely; nirbahsam- illuminating; svarupa – own form; sunyam – empty, void, lacking; iva- as if samadhih- continuous effortless linking o f the attention to a higher concentration force or person.

*That same effortless linkage of the attention when experienced as illumination of the higher concentration force or person, while the yogi feels as if devoid of himself, is Samadhi or continuous effortless linkage of his attention to the special Person, object, or force.*

## Commentary:

Samadhi is not defined here as it is popularly described by so many meditation authorities by those who dislike it or shun it as being impersonal. There is no word here that says that Samadhi is a void or that it is sunya. The word sunya occurs in reference to the svarupa or form of the yogi, and on in the sense while he is in contact with the force, object or person of his interest, he is so much connected to it that his own forms seems as if it were not there and that only the force object or other person being contacted was there. The Sanskrit article iva means "as if". When there is continued effortless linkage of the attention to a higher concentration force, object or person, the yogi's attention is completely or near completely given over to that higher reality, so that it feels as if he is not there (iva sunya) and that only the higher reality is present with illumination (nirbhasam). This gives him a thorough insight into the said force, object or person.

# Verse 4

trayam ekatra sanyamah

**trayam- three; ekatra- in one place, all taken together as one practice; samyamah- complete restraint**

*The three as one practice is the complete restraint.*

## Commentary:

In Bhagavad-gita, samyama is mentioned in chapter four.

*srotradini `ndriyany anye*

*samyamagnisu juhvati*

*sabdadin visayan anye*

*indriyagnisu juhvati*

Other yogis offer hearing and other sensual powers into the fiery power of restraint. Some offer sound and other sensual pursuits into the fiery sensual power. (Gita 4.26)

*sarvani'ndriya karmani*

*pranakarmani capare*

*atmasamyama yogagnau*

*juhvati jnanadipite*

Some ascetics subject the sensual actions and the breath function to self-restraint by fiery yoga austerities, which are illuminated by experience. (Gita 4.27) Sam means very, quite, greatly, thoroughly, very much, all, whole, complete. Yamah means restraint, control. It is obvious that one has to understand the word according to how it is defined by the particular writer. Sri Krishna's use of the term is similar to what Sri Patanjali meant, but Sri Patanjali is specific in saying that samyama is the combining the three practices of higher yoga into one discipline. When dharana, dhyana and Samadhi are made into one technique, that is called samyamah in Sri Patanjali's vocabulary. From that perspective, there would be only 6 stages to yoga, namely yama, niyama, asana, pranayama, pratyahar, and samyamah. In that case samyamah means that one has to do the three higher stages of yoga as one practice. This actually happens when one masters dhyana yoga. Sometimes in dhyana, one slips back to the dharana stages and sometimes it progresses automatically to the Samadhi stage. Thus Sri Patanjali is correct in bridging the three higher stages when there is success in this, the mento-emotional energy is completely restrained from its involvement in this world and in the lower subtle world.

# Verse 7

**trayam antarangam purvebhyah**

trayam- three; antarangam= antar- internal, psychological, concerning the thinking and feeling organs + angam- part purvebhyah, in reference to the preliminary stages mentioned before.

*In reference to the preliminary stages of yoga, these three higher states concern the psychological organs.*

**Commentary:**

Dharana, dhyana and Samadhi concern the psychological organs. These concern mystic practice as assisted by the physical and social practices which involve yama, niyama, asana, pranayama and pratyahar. While in the five preliminary stages there are physical actions, in the three higher stages, it is mostly mystic actions having to do with controlling, observing and operating psychological organs in the subtle body.

# Verse 8

### tad api bahirangam nirbijasya

**tadapi= that = api – even; bahiranga= bahir- external +angam – part; nirbijasya- not motivated by the mento-emotional energy**

### Commentary:

Initially a student yogi works for yoga success on the basis of disgust with the subtle and gross material energy. It is due to the impressions lodged in his mental and emotional energies. Thus in a sense he cannot strive without being motivated by those very same energies. As Sri Patanjali told us, the purpose of that energy is to give us experience in the world and also to do the converse which is to motivate us to strive for liberation. *prakasa-kriya-sthiti-silam bhutendriyatmakam bhogapavargartham drsyam* What is perceived is of the nature of the mundane elements and the sense organs and is formed in clear perception, action or stability. Its purpose is to give experience or to allow liberation. (Yoga Sutra 2:18) While initially the student yogi practices samyama complete restrain under motivations which comes from the mental end emotional energies, later on , as he advances, he progresses on the basis of forces objects and personas he encounters in the spiritual atmosphere. Such motivations are free from flaws. These are termed seedless or lacking urges from this side of existence.

# Verse 9

**vyutthana-nirodha-sanskarayor abhibhava-pradhurbhavan nirodha-kshanachittanvayo nirodha-parinamah**

vyutthana- expression; nirodha – suppression; samskarayoh- of the mento-emotional impressions; abhibhava- disappearance; pradurbhavau- and manifestation ; nirodha- restraint, cessation ; ksana-momentarily; citta - mento-emotional energy; anvayah- connection; nirodah- restraint; parinamah-= transforming effects

*When the connection with the citta mento-emotional energy momentarily ceases during the manifestation and disappearance phases when there is expression or suppression of the impressions, that is the restraint of the transforming mento-emotional energy.*

## Commentary:

Sri Patanjali is respect by all advanced yogis who are aware of these yoga sutras. Only persons who do no yoga and who are ignorant of the techniques, make a joke of the detailed work of Sri Patanjali. One can only admire his genius. There are many who become masters of kriya yoga. Most of them do not take detailed notes of the preliminary and advanced practices. This is because those yogis are to liberated and do not see the need to keep a record for review. However Sri Patanjali saw the need. This is a detailed study of his practices. I offer respects to him. A student yogi should note what is emotional and what is mental energy. He should note that the two energies are interchangeable under certain psychological circumstances. Furthermore even though the mental energy hold to its own integrity, showing a distinction between itself and the emotions, still the two energies do communicate with each other. Beyond that, a student should note how impressions arise and subside. Anyone who has done concentration, contemplation or meditation, knows very well that the impressions come and go of their own accord. But Sri Patanjali spoke of the interval (ksana) between the expression of an idea in the mind and the suppression of that very same idea. At first this sounds easy. But let us think of it again. When an idea arises in the mind, depending on it's value to the emotions, it may be expanded or it may be dissipated immediately. If it is expanded, what really takes place? If it is expanded the idea ceases for a split second. The memory in conjunction with the imagination creates another idea which is associative to the one which disappeared. Sri Patanjali wants us to focus on that split second cessation (nirodhaksana ). He wants us to extend that split second to a longer, much longer period. If we could keep the mind in that state for long we would enter into samadhi. Of course such a feat is easier said than done. Sometimes effortlessly, the mind remains for five or ten seconds in that blank state. Expert yogis hold the mind in that state for minutes and some do so for hours at a time. This is their accomplishment of samadhi. One will find that if he can hold the mind there, the imagination faculty will change into being spiritual vision, an actual illuminating sight, an eye. With the help of Lord Krishna, Arjuna had some experiences of this at Kuruksetra. When again Arjuna wanted that insight, Sri Krishna with mild disappointment, declined. He said, in the Anugita, that He could not again impart it to Arjuna because it involved a yoga siddhai which Krishna expressed at Kurukshetra for a specific purpose. By careful study of this verse, one will get an idea of what is required for yoga success, which is the prolonging of the momentary blankness which occurs in the mind between the expression within it of one idea and another. The whole problem with meditation has to do with this. For success, a yogi must be prepared to spend years if necessary noticing that momentarily blankness and practicing to hold the mind there. Initially, it will seem that it is impossible to stop the mind there, but by regular practice for a long time, the period for holding the mind in that state is extended.

# Verse 10

tasya prashanta-vahita sanskarat

tasya- of this; prasanta- spiritual peace; vahita- flow; samskarat- from the impressioins derrived

*Concerning this practice of restraint, the impressions derived cause a flow of spiritual peace.*

### Commentary:

When the yogi repeated practices to keep his mind in a condition of restraining, causing the transformations of the mento-emotional energy to cease, then his memory is accredited with quieting impressions, which bring on the uninterrupted flow of spiritual peace.

# Verse 11

sarvarthataikagratayoh kshayodayau chittasya samadhi-parinamah

sarvarthata - varying objective; ekagratayoh - of the one aspect before the attention; ksaya – decrease; udayau- and increase; cittasya – of the mento-emotional energy; samadhi- the continuous effortless linkage of the attention to the higher concentration force, object or person; parinamah - transforming effects, change

*The decrease of varying objectives in the mento-emotional energy and the increase of the one aspect within it, is the change noticed in the practice of continuous effortless effor of linking the attention to higher concentration forces, objects or persons.*

## Commentary:

We are reminded that the samadhi stage will come after long practice. It will come gradually over time of practicing Samyama, as Sri Patanjali defined, being the practice of dharana which progressed into dhyana, which then changes into samadhi. As one tries to practice samadhi, he will find that there is a decrease in the minds many objectives and an increase of its tendency for one focus as dictated by the practice. This one focus is not a focus on a deity but rather it is the focus mentioned in verse 9 of this chapter, which is the restraint of the transformations of the mento-emotional energy. It has nothing to do with any object or any person, divine or ordinary. It is a battle within the psychology of the yogi, for control of the psyche. It is an internal private war in the battlefield of the mind and emotions. When the yogin notices that his mind's habits change, so that it desires more of that peace attained when it is in a void state, then he knows that he is making progress. This is not a void in the world nor in the subtle world but rather a void in his own psyche, whereby his memory does not discharge ideas which burst in the mind environment into impressions which trigger other impressions and thoughts and which torment the yogi and frustrate his efforts and psyche control.

# Verse 12

tatah punah shantoditau tulya-pratyayau chittasyaikagrataparinamah

tatah- then; punah – again; santoditau = santa -tranquilized, settled, subsided + uditau - and agitated, emerging; tulya – similar; pratyayau - conviction or belief as mental content, instinctive interest; cittasya - of the mento-emotional energy; ekagrata- of what is in front of one aspect before the attention; parinamah- transforming effects, change

*Then again, when the mind's content is the same as it was when it is subsiding and when it is emerging, that is the transformation called "having one aspect in front before the attention".*

## Commentary:

This condition of mind is related to everything which was described in this chapter so far. As the yogin gets to the stage where his mind content is no longer dominated by memories, he is able to keep before his attention in a quiescent state, (prasanta - vahita verse 9). However this is maintained only by keeping the expressive and depressive restraining gyration of the mind out of contact with the memory. At any time, when the mind is allowed to contact the attention is allowed to contact the memory, either by accident or as induced or deliberately, the mind content will be altered to accommodate various images and sounds (sarvathata, verse 11). That is counter productive, being regretted by the yogi, since it puts him at odds with his objective, which is to cease such mental operations completely.

The subsiding and emerging nature of the mind cannot be changed but a yogi can get relief from it by his assumption of a focus into other dimensions and by his freezing the mind by pranayama practice. But as soon as it is possible, the mind will be found to have reverted back to its essential nature. This is in a sense disgusting and it causes the yogin to feel that somehow he has got to get rid of such a mind.

It is not easy to have just one aspect in front of the attention. By nature the mind seeks to change its position by an in and out sising and falling, creating and disintegrating function. This is the natural condition of the normal mindal stage. This is why it is necessary to do pranayama. By regulating the breath and by surcharging the mind with a high pressure charge of prana, it slows down or abandons lower diversions altogether. But then again as soon as the higher pressure charge dissipates, the mind returns to its normal gyrations, except in the case of those yogins who have developed a yoga siddha body. Skeptics therefore suspect that yoga is a waste of time. They feel that no one can overcome the gyrating nature of the mind. For the mind content to be the same when the mento-emotional energy is moving to create images as to disintegrate the same and for the mind to remain consistently blank like this for sometime, the yogin has to master the dharana, sixth stage of yoga practice, whereby he can link the mind to a consistent concentration force and at the same time hold on to or look through his attention energy.

The technique used for this is the one where the yogi keeps his attention locked to the subtle sound which comes in from the chit akash. Usually that is heard in the vicinity of the right ear. As a yogi hears this, he also focuses on diffused light in front of him (ekagrata). There is no visual object before his attention at this time. It is merely a listening to the naad sound in the vacinity of the right ear, while looking forward through his attention which makes a slight contact with the mento-emotional energy (citta). When his looking action relaxes of its own accord, he sees a diffused light before him.

Sri Patanjali already mentioned that diffusion as a covering of light. That was in Verse 52 of the last chapter.

### *tatah ksiyate prakasa-avaranam*

From that is dissipated, the mental darkness which veils the light. (Yoga Sutra 2.52)

The diffused light which is actually light mixed with cloudy energy or misty force, will be separated such that the misty force or cloudy energy will disappear, leaving only light. When a yogi attains this practice, it is understood that he mastered the seventh state of yoga called dhyana.

Some people think that this practice includes imagining a deity, a supernatural, or spiritual being, or imaging a subtle primal force, but that is incorrect. The yogi only needs to get his supernatural and spiritual visions to be operative. Then he sees everything in the chit akash, the sky of consciousness. H does not need to imagine anything super-subtle or divine objects.

# Verse 13

etena bhutendriyeshu dharma-lakshanavastha-parinama vyakhyatah

etena- by this; bhuta – the various states of matter; indiryesu- by the sensual energy; dharma- quality; laksana – shape, characteristic; avastha-condition; parinamah – changes, transformation; vyakhyatah – is described

*By this description of the changes, the quality, shape, changing conditions of the various states of mater and the sensual energy was described.*

## Commentary:

The whole subtle and gross material energy is effectively dealt with th this yoga practice, in the efforts of the yogi to get his psychology under control. The whole controlling effort has to do with the developing a complete disinterest in the gross and subtle material energy, which is called bhutendiriya in this verse. Our response to the mundane energy is out down fall. When we learn how to control that response and how to eventually cease responding altogether, we will get the control which we so desperately seek.

# Verse14

shantoditavyapadeshya-dharmanupati dharmi

aanta – collapsed; udita- emergent; avyapadesya – what is not to be defined, what is latent; dharma – law, sustaining force; anupati – reach full retrogression; dharmi – most basic condition

*When the collapsed, emergent and latent forces reach full retrogression, that is the most basic condition.*

## Commentary:

Most commentators attribute dharmi as the prakriti energy, or the most subtle form of material nature. This is correct. However, in the case of the yogi, his research into it has to do with finding a technique for abandoning it once and for all, for complete detachment and independence from it. Thus the assessment of it occurs within his psyche within the mentoemotional energy. Once he gets down to its most basic condition, or to the ultimate substratum of material nature, he can take a good look at it with supernatural vision and make his decisions for not responding to it anymore. Once he sees the course of its progression into manifestation, and retrogression out of manifestation, he will no longer be afraid of it or be attracted to it. Then it served its purpose for him and he becomes liberated quickly and definitely.

Obviously we have got some desire to be in touch with material energy. Thus it is necessary that we understand our attraction to it and eliminate that fondness for it or eradicate and dismember whatever it is that influenced us to embrace it.

# Verse 15

kramanyatvam parinamanyatve hetuh

**krama – sequence; anyatvam- otherness, difference; parinama-transformation change; anyatve – in difference; hetuh – cause**

*The cause of a difference in the transformation is the difference in the sequential changes.*

## Commentary:

A student yogi may become preoccupied with the various changing scenes which occur when the mento-emotional energy (citta) goes through its numerous operations. Thus he becomes bewildered, but sooner or later he will get help from a senior yogin, such that he will no longer follow the sequential changes but will instead observe the operations of the energy. The content of the operations is not important. He has to grasp this fact, if he is to acquire supreme detachment and get leverage over the transformations which occur in his mind and emotions and which keep him from achieving the supernatural and spiritual insights. Some student yogins like infants, become spell bound by their imagination faculty and its picturizations. They make little progress in higher yoga and talk about it to their teachers. They need to understand that a fascination with the differences, in the various transformations is caused only by differences in the sequential changes and not from any thing substantial or meaningful. Whatever occurs in their sill little minds is of no consequence really. It is not the content of the mind (pratyaya), nor the conviction or moody appetite of the mind that is relevant but rather the way the mind operates.

A person entering a film theater usually becomes enthralled in what show is on the screen. But that is childish. He should be interested in the projector mechanism which causes the movie to be shown in the first place. It is the working of that mechanism that is important, not the content of the various movies which are shown through it. When a student yogi gets this understanding, he becomes freed. So long as one is attracted primarily to the mind content, one will not adhere to the instructions for higher yoga, but will instead, complain about the disciplines just as how a child cries if his parent takes him out of a movie theater before a film is finished.

The parent wants to show the child the projection apparatus and the operator of that mechanism, but the child finds the projection room to be dull and boring and not as stimulating as the film show it produces. He feels that it is not interactive with him. So the student yogi usually fights tooth and nail with advanced teachers who come down from siddhaloka to free them.

The difference in the sequential change of ideas and images in the mind occur because of how the memory and imagination interact with the information which comes in a compressed form from the senses from the subtle and gross world. This admixture is bewildering. Advanced yogis advise us to forgo them, to just ignore them. Their policy is that instead of looking at those impressions, we should just avoid them all together. This avoidance is disempowered them and weakens their grip on us.

The analogy of the boy in the movie house would help in this case. The more and more he stays out of the movie house, the more detached and disinterested he may become, the more he goes to it, the more his nature reacts in response to it and the more attached and interested he becomes. But in that case his interest is being abused, being needlessly exploited by fiction. This is why in India, there was a period of history where many leading yogis condemned human consumption of name and forms. If we become enthralled again and again with names of things and with the forms of things, it will cause us to become more and more fascinated with this world and that will push us away from liberation.

According to the sequence of the various film slides, the movie shows in particular ways which may invoke our interest, either to cause happiness, distress or indifference, and according to how the memory, imagination, reasoning and sensual intake interact, we become fascinated with the differences in the transformation within our minds and emotions. Thus the important thing is to understand how the mind operates, not what the content of it comprises. Even though this is the solution, this is easier said than done. When one becomes determined to follow this advice, he discovers that somehow he is enthralled by the content of the mind. That itself entraps him. At least that is how a student yogin will feel. But again, he should study the operation of the entrapment mechanism.

The boy in our analogy must study how the movie building was constructed with a small door for entry on a back street and a large attractive door for entry on a main street. The very construction of the place is bewildering and causes the body to go into the theater through the front door, which leads into the gallery where the movie is showing. Once the boy understands this he can avoid that door and find his way to the small door on the back street which leads to the projection room where he will be able to study something that is of vital importance to him, which is the way the projection apparatus operates.

Sometimes a student yogi finds that he repeatedly finds himself in front of a series of images which are projected by the imagination faculty or which were released from the memory or from the sensual organs which collect information. Before he can realize it, or be objective to it, he finds himself looking, analyzing, interacting with these images. This procedure, though impulsive must be stopped by the student yogin.

# Verse 16

**parinama-traya-sanyamad atitanagata-jnanam**

parinama – transformation change; traya - threefold; samyamat- from the complete restraint of the mento-emotional energy; atita – past; anagata- future; jnanam- information

*From the complete restrain of the mento-emotional energy in terms of the three-fold transformations within it, the yogi gets information about the past and future.*

## Commentary:

This set of verses regarding the perfectional skills or siddhis gained by certain practices, have caused Sri Patanjali to be criticized by those religious leaders who feel that the siddhi perfectional powers are a distraction either from liberation or from attaining love of God. However, the accusation is ungrounded, because Sri Patanjali very realistically informs us about the course of our development, alerting us to what lies ahead. These perfectional skills cannot be avoided by anyone who advances in spiritual disciplines. We need training in how not to be charmed by these powers of the lower and higher subtle bodies. Everything about the past in microscopic and atomic impressions is in our individual memories and in the cosmic memory pool. Any of this information can be retrieved by the Supreme Being.

**sri bhagavan uvaca**

**bahuni me vyatitani**

**janmani tava ca'rjuna**

**tanyaham veda sarvani**

**na tvam vettha paramtapa**

The Blessed Lord said: Many of My births transpired, and yours, Arjuna. I recall them all.

*You do not remember, O scorcher of the enemies. (Gita 4.5)*

Everything about the future is potential present in the existence right now. The parameters which will cause the formation of the future are present. The Supreme Being can look at it and accurately gage the probabilities.

On should not interpret this verse to mean that a yogi can know just about everything. A yogi can know much if he applies himself sufficiently and can enter into the cosmic memory and decipher its impressions. First of all, he must be allowed to do that. This allowance is not always grated to a yogi by the Supreme Being. However a yogi does not need the permission of the Supreme Being to enter his own limited memory bank. His ability to do that relies on his expertise in the complete restrain of his mento-emotional energy.

A great yogin, Shrila Yogeshwarananda can decipher the cosmic parameters which will control what happens in the future of this universe. Therefore it is possible but only a rare yogin can do this. The complete conquest of the mento-emotional energy is a feat reserved for a select few great yogis like him. The important achievement is to get your own memory under control. When this is done one can check on the relationship between one limited memory and the cosmic reservoir of past impressions.

Some people feel that if a yogi reaches a stage of knowledge about the past and future, he would be omniscient, but that is an exaggeration. Such information will not affect the course of history nor change any of the probability, nor affect how the Supreme Being relates to the limited personalities. Its value is in the potency to convince the yogi to make an exit from these gross and subtle mundane histories. But that is not all, because a yogin has to acquire permission to do that. That permission must be gained from the Supreme Being, who might not grant it to a particular yogin.

# Verse 17

shabdartha-pratyayanam itaretaradhyasat sankaras tat-
pravibhagasanyamat sarva-bhuta-ruta-jnanam

sabda – sound; artha – meaning; pratayayam – pertaining to the mind
content, convictions, idea; itaretara = itara -it + tara = one for the other;
adhyasat- resulting from the super-imposition; sankarah – intermixture;
tat – their; pravibhaga – differentiation, sorting, classification, mental
clarity; samyamat – from the complete restraint of the mento-emotional
energy; sarva – all; bhuta – creature; ruta – sound, cry, yell, language;
jnanam- information, knowledge

*From the complete restraint of the mento emotional energy In relation
to mental clarity, regarding the intermixture resulting from the
superimposition one for the other, of sound, it's meaning and the related
mentality, knowledge about the language of all creatures is gained*

## Commentary:

When a student yogin simplifies his mentality by sorting out the various parts
of it, and when he detaches his imagination faculty from it's involuntary
connection to the memory, as well as when he consistently retracts his sensual
energies from the gross and lower suble worlds, he gains a certain mental
clarity, by which his buddhi organ instanteously sorts the sound, it's meaning
and related idea which was made by any other creature.

# Verse 18

sanskara-sakshatkaranat purva-jatijnanam

samskara- the subtle impressions stored in memory; sakstkaranata- fear causing to be visibly present, direct intuitive perception; purva- before, previous; jati - status, life; jananam- knowledge

*From direct intuitive perception of the subtle impressions stored in the memory, the yogi gains knowledge of previous lives.*

## Commentary:

A yogi may know his own or some past lives of others. He can intuit into the memory the impressions and pull up from there the compressed information, which can be instantly translated by his purified buddhi organ.

# Verse 19

### pratyayasya para-chitta-jnanam

pratyayasya – of the mind content; para- of others; citta – of the mento-emotional energy jnanam- information

*A yogi can know the contents of the mental and emotional energy in the mind of others.*

### Commentary:

Even though a student yogi might experience this, he must check the purity of his buddhi organ to be sure that his intuition has interpreted accurately. He should not inform others that he has this ability. Unless he gets directions from Lord Shiva or from an advanced yogi, he should not disclose to others anything about his intuitions. Generally, a yogi should not interfere with the lives of others, for he should be aware of the supervision of the supernatural persons like Lord Krishna and Lord Vishnu.

# Verse 20

**na cha tat salambanam tasyavishayi-bhutatvat**

na- not; ca- and; tat – that; salambananam- leaning on, resting on, support; tasya – of that; avisayi- not an object of anything , imperceptible; bhutavat- the actual object

*And he does not check a factor which is the support of that content, for it is not the actual object in question.*

# Verse 21

kaya-rupa-sanyamat tad-grahya-shakti-stambhe
chakshuhprakashasanprayoge 'ntardhanam

kaya- body; rupa – form; samyamat- from the complete restraint of the mento-emotional energy; tat – that; sakti- power, potency, energy; stambhe- on the suspension; caksuh- vision; prakasa – light; samprayoge – on not contacting; antardhanam+ antardhanam= invisibility

*From the complete restraint of the mento-emotional energy in relation to the shape of the body, on the suspension of the receptive energy, there is no contact between light and vision, which results in invisibility.*

## Commentary:

The mento-emotional energy emanates a psychic light which is called an aura. Now if this aura is restrained or if it loses its expressiveness the particular form cannot be seen by another.

A yogi may also suspend this energy from operating. In that case, others who send out psychic feelers to find him, discover to their dismay that he is missing. Sometimes when this happens, the persons who are trying to find that yogi know that he is in the vicinity or that he is where they think he is, therefore they become annoyed and attribute the lack of contact to his anti-social tendency.

The lack of contact (samprayoga) between the light and vision has to do with the light coming from the yogi's form and vision beam which emanates from the person who searches physically for him. Sometimes a yogi can sit right next to a person and that person cannot realize that the yogi is by his side. One of my gurus, a certain Rishi Singh Gherwal was hired by the British government to find himself. Being employed as a spy to find a spy he remained in the services of the British for many years. He was a mahayogi but was unknown because of his great humility and resistance to popularity.

# Verse 22

## etena sthabdady antardhanam uktam

etena – by this; sabdadi = sabda – sound+ adi- and the related sensual pursuits andardhanam- invisibility, non- perceptibility; uktam – described

*By this method, sound and the related sensual pursuits, may be restrained, which results in the related perceptibility.*

### Commentary:

A yogi may use a mystic process to cause imperceptibility in any or all aspects of sensual energy, so that he may not be detected by others. But this might only be done for the sake of yoga practice progression, and not otherwise. If a yogi uses these mystic skills for other reasons, it will distract from yoga practice and cause a long or short lapse in progression. Sometimes people send out thoughts to attract a yogi. They do this by thinking. These thoughts are transmitted from their hearts just like radio waves being transmitted from a radio station. These thoughts are usually disruptive to yoga practice and are usually meant to engage a yogi in cultural activities which do not accelerate, but which rather decelerate yoga. Thus a yogi has to protect his practice by causing such thoughts not to reach him. There are many ways of doing this. The yogi uses a method, which he is allowed according to the level of his practice.

Just as a yogi might sit next to someone on a bus or train and travel miles with that person, without the person recognizing him, even though he is the very same person whom that searcher seeks, so a yogi might stay out of reach of the others even though he might be right next to them or even though they might know him so well that their thoughts instantly reach his psyche.

# Verse 23

sopakramam nirupakramam cha karma tat-sanyamad aparanta-
jnanam arishtebhyo va

sopakrama-set about, undertaken, already operative; nirupakramam-
dormant-destined; ca- and; karma- cultural activities; tat- that;
samyamad= samyamat-from the complete restraint of the mento-
emotional energy; aparanta- of the other end, of death entry into the
hereafter; jananam- knowledge; aristebhyo+ aristebhah- from portents;
va- or

*Complete restraint of the mento-emotional energy in relation to current
and destined cultural activities results in knowledge of entry into the
hereafter. Or the same result is gained by the complete restraint in relation
to portents.*

## Commentary:

Both the current and the future cultural activities are the result of destiny,
which is a combination of several forces. These destined energies work now,
they worked in the past. They will work in the future. By restraining the mento-
emotional energy in relation to the confusing impressions which we take in
now, and the ones which are stored in our memory we may derive intuitive or
direct supernatural perceptions into the subtle world to see when it would be
necessary for any of us to leave a material body. By this process, a yogi can
leave his body and enter the dimensions of the hereafter where civilizations
are currently taking place. Each person who is about to leave his or her body
experiences portents. Most persons cannot properly interpret the indications.
A yogi can accurately gage those signs and messages.

# Verse 24

maitry-adishu balani

**maitri-** friendliness; **adisu-** and by related qualities; **balani-** power

*By complete restraint of the mento-emotional energy in relation to friendliness he develops that very same power.*

## Commentary:

When the yogi detaches himself from the cultural prejudices which were cultivated in this and in some past lives, he develops universal friendliness which is applied evenly without biases which come up from the subconscious memory as predispositions. However, being aware of those attitudes in his memory, he can know what sort of friendly or antagonistic relationship he had with others in past lives.

# Verse 25

baleshu hasti-baladini

**balesu**- by strength; **hasti**- elephant; **bala**- strength; **adina**- and the same for other aspects

*By complete restraint of the mento-emotional energy in relation to strength, the yogin acquires strength of an elephant. The same applies to other aspects.*

## Commentary:

A yogi develops certain mystic perfections during practice. This cannot be avoided. A yogi must stick to his objectives as shared with him by advanced teachers. Then he is not distracted by the mystic perfection, but observes their development and notes the various powers of the subtle and super-subtle bodies.

# Verse 26

pravritty-aloka-nyasat sukshma-vyavahita-viprakrishta-jnanam

pravrttyalokanyasat= pravrtti- destined activity, the force of cultural activity+ aloka – supernatural insight + nyasat – from placing or applying; suksma – subtle; vyavhita- concealed; viprakrsta- concealed; viprakrsta- remote; jnanam – knowledge

*From the application of supernatural insight to the force producing cultural activities, a yogi gets information about what is subtle, concealed and what is remote from him.*

## Commentary:

Sometimes it is necessary to side step destiny and to see what will happen if one takes one kind of action or if one stays in a particular dimension or world. Then a yogi might apply supernatural vision to peer into the future, so that he can make a decision to remain in one dimension or be transcribed into another. A yogi can only find out what he is allowed to by the Supreme Being, but that allowance is very wide. He may get special insight from Lord Shiva or from some other diving being.

# Verse 27

bhavana-jnanam surye sanyamat

bhuvana- the solar system; jnana- knowledge; surye- on the sun-god or the sun planet samyamat- from the complete restraint of the mento-emotional energy

*From the complete restraint of the mento-emotional energy in relation to the sun god or the sun planet, knowledge of the solar system is gained.*

## Commentary:

If for some reason or the other, a yogi wants to know about the jurisdictional influences of the sun-god or sun planet, he may find out if he applies his spiritual sight to the spiritual, supernatural, or gross influences of the sunlight. The sun god's influence abounds physically, supernaturally, and spiritually as well. This is why Sri Krishna described the paths used by proficient yogis at the time of death.

yatra kale tv anavrttim

avrttim cai 'va yoginah

prayata yanti tam kalam

vaksyami bharatarsabha

O bullish man of the Bharata family, I will tell you of the departure for the yogis

who do or do not return. (Gita 8.23)

agnir jyotir ahah suklah

sanmasa uttarayanam

tatra prayata gacchanti

brahma brahmavido janah

The summer season, the bright atmosphere, the daytime, the bright moonlight, the six months when the sun appears to move north; if at that time, they depart the body, those people who know the spiritual dimension, go to the spiritual location.

(Gita 8.24)

dhumo ratris tatha krsnah

sanmasa daksinayanam

tatra candramasam jyotir

yogi prapya nivartate

The smoky, misty or hazy season, as well as in the night-time, the dark-moon time, the six months when the sun appears to move south; if the yogi departs at that time, he attains moonlight, after which he is born again. (Gita 8.25)

suklakrsne gati hy ete

jagatah sasvate mate

ekaya yaty anavrttim

anyaya'vartate punah

**The tight and the dark times are two paths which are considered to be perpetually available for the universe. It is considered so by the authorities. By one, a person goes away not to return; by the other he comes back again. (Gita 8.26)**

# Verse 28

chandre tara-vyuha-jnanam

candre- on the moon or moon-god; tara- stars; vyuha- system; jnanam- knowledge

*By complete restraint of the mento-emotional energy, in reference to moon or moon-god, the yogi gets knowledge about the system of stars.*

### Commentary:

This is in the case of a yogi who has an interest of going beyond the jurisdiction of the solar deity. To relieve himself of reliance on this person, a yogi must get permission for transference to another zone of some other deity. All places are controlled. Thus a yogi needs permission both to leave this realm as well as to enter any other.

A yogi's desire for something is not guaranteed that he will acquire it. It all depends on if he is permitted and if he qualified by the required austerities. Yogis who are spiritually linked to a local deity like the sun-god or moon-god, cannot relinquish their spiritual connection, even though they may get permission for a change of services or for a relocation to another zone that is controlled by the same deity.

# Verse 29

**dhruve tad-gati-jnanam**

dhruve- on the Pole ?Star; tat- that; gati – course of heavenly planets and stars; jnanam- knowledge

*By the complete restrain of the mento-emotional energy in relation to the Pole Star, a yogi can know of the course of planets and stars.*

## Commentary:

Some yogis do develop whimsical interest and inquiries which satisfy their curiosity. But other yogis who are serious about it and who hope to migrate from this planet to other superior places do check on the other zones before leaving their bodies, to be sure that their conceptions of these places perfectly match the actual situations there. Such yogis use their higher astral bodies to move from sphere to sphere checking the various living conditions in the other places.

# Verse 30

nabhi-chakre kaya-vyuha-jnanam

nabhi – navel; cakre- on the energy gyrating center; kaya- body; vyuha – arrangement, lay out; jnanam- knowledge

*By complete restraint of the mento-emotional energy in relation to the focusing on the navel energy gyrating center, the yogi gets knowledge about the layout of his body.*

## Commentary:

It is necessary in the course of kundalini yoga to energize the energy gyrating centers or chakras. These are located on the spinal column in the subtle body. This corresponds to the central nervous system in the gross form. The navel chakra point extends to the front of the body, to the solar plexus region. In the case of student yogis, it may also point downward. But in advanced celibate yogis it points upwards.

A yogin may enter the navel chakra of his own body or that of others, from the front of the body, from the navel, where the umbilical cord was connected while that body was in the womb of the it's mother. From there a yogi can see the entire layout of the body, including its life spans, its potential for disease and its maximum capacity for helping the soul in the quest for liberation.

In some cases, a person cannot be liberated in his present body. When a yogi sees this he does not waste time with that person. He directs that person to earn more conducive birth opportunities. In yogic terminology the navel chakra is called manipuraka. It is the third major chakra when counting these from the bottom of the spine. By completing the course of hatha yoga, a yogi curbs this chakra.

# Verse 31

## kantha-kupe kshut-pipasa-nivrittih

**kantha-** throat; **kupe** – on the gullet; **ksut-** hunger; **pipasa-** thirst; **nivrttih-** cessation, suppression

*By the complete restraint of the mento-emotional energy in focusing on the gullet, a yogi causes the suppression of hunger and thirst.*

### Commentary:

The practice of suppressing hunger and thirst is part of Hatha yoga. The purpose of this is to get the life force to cease its independent activities. A hatha yogi endeavors to bring the life force under his control, not to stop it from functioning but to cease its independent activities which are counter productive to the aims of yoga. Thus one, by one, a yogi surcharges and subsequently purifies the energy gyrating centers (chakras) one by one, beginning at the base of the spine.

Some people feel that they can use raja yoga to purify the chakras from the top downwards, from the brow or crown chakra. Actually this cannot be done, except in a person's imagination. One has to do kundalini yoga by a vigor practice like bhastrika pranayama. By charging the body with prana and pushing it down into the passages which are filled with apana, one causes purification from the base chakra upwards. It takes a certain amount of practice according to the extent of impurities.

A yogi does cause his hunger and thirst to be suppressed initially when he sets out to control those urges, but over a time of practice, his subtle body changes and the urges for solid and liquid food go away. This is because the attitude of the throat chakras become changed permanently.

Of course a yogi can be degraded, because whatever low habits or vices he acquired in the past, he can again take up in the future if he is not careful, or if he is not transferred into a dimension where such sordid aspects are unavailable.

# Verse 32

**kurma-nadyam sthairyam**

**kurma-** tortoise, a particular subtle nerve; **nadyam** –on the nadi or subtle nerve; **sthairyam-** steadiness

*By the complete restraint of the mento-emotional energy in focusing on the kurmanadi subtle nerve, a yogi acquires steadiness of his psyche.*

## Commentary:

This has to do with being ready to enter Samadhi which is continuous effortless linkage of one's attention to a higher concentration force, object or person. Unless one can keep his body in a steady pose, preferably the padmasana lotus posture, and also have the bodily urges like hunger quelled completely, he cannot enter into samadhi. Sri Patanjali brings this to our attention at this point.

The kurmanadi is supposed to be located below the gullet. In other words if one has not stilled the gross and subtle nerves in this area, having mastered Hatha Yoga, one will not be able to enter samadhi. When those nerves are stilled, the life force gives up its effort to protect and overly maintain the lower part of the body, the part which is lower than the neck. Unless the life force can be relieved from its creature survival duties, it does not allow the person to enter samadhi.

# Verse 33

## murdha-jyotishi siddha-darshanam

**murdha – the head; jyotisi- on the shinning light; siddha- the perfected being; darsanam- the view of**

*By the complete restraint of the mento-emotional energy as it is focused on the shinning light in the head of the subtle body, a yogi gets views of the perfected beings.*

### Commentary:

Murdhajyotish is known otherwise as jnanadipa or jnanadiptih or jnanachaksu. It is a light seen in the front central head of the subtle body. This light is the energized buddhi organ. In its normal stage in a human being, it is dark and cloudy, like a filament of a light bulb which gets insufficient current. The insufficient current warms the filament but does not cause it to glow noticeable. When the yogi masters pranayama and perfects himself in the disciplines of kundalini and celibacy yoga, his buddhi organ gets sufficiently charged. It glows with shining light (jyotisi), otherwise it remains dull but is felt as the centre of the mind, as ones ability to understand, analyses, plan and draw conclusions.

When a yogi develops himself to the extent that his buddhi organ begins to glow in his lower subtle body even, then he perceives the perfected beings, the siddhas like Sri Babaji Mahasya, Sri Gorakshanath, and other Mahayogins. Sometimes fortunately he sees Lord Shiva at Kailash in the other dimensions. Once a yogin sees the siddhas, it is understood that he is blessed. If he accelerates the practice further, he will develop a yoga siddha body. He can take advices and get rare kriya yoga practices from those siddhas whom he is allowed to perceive. Such a yogin does not rely on physical contact with a yoga guru. Hence he does not have to have a guru who uses a physical form. He takes initiation either physically or subtle from these teachers.

# Verse 34

pratibhad va sarvam

pratibhat- resulting from Samyama on the shinning organ of divination; va- or; sarvam- everything, all reality

*By complete restraint of the mento-emotional energy while focusing on the shining organ of divination in the head of the subtle body, the yogin gets the ability to know all reality.*

## Commentary:

This pratibha is the brahmarandra development in the head of the subtle body of a yogi. At first a yogi develops the top part of the subtle body which is known as the brahmarandra. Sri Patanjali used the terms, pratibha which literally means relating to divination or genius. A yogi who has developed his brahmarandra is said to be liberated even while using a gross body. Such a yogi can select which of the dimensions he would live in after he sheds his material body, but of course again, since he is a limited being in the conditioned and liberated stages, he has to get approval from higher authorities like Lord Shiva or Lord Krishna.

# Verse 35

hridaye chitta-sanvit

hrdaye- on the samyam on the causal body; citta- mento-emotional energy; samvit- thorough insight

*By the complete restraint of the mento-emotional energy as it is focused on the causal body in the vicinity of the chest, the yogi gets thorough insight into the cause of the mental and emotional energy.*

## Commentary:

For all these practices, one should have mastered the samyama procedure described before by Sri Patanjali as a development from dharana, to dhyana and to Samadhi. Once this is mastered, one can apply himself to the practices described. Stated differently on who mastered samdhi can use Samadhi.

A person whose mind is jumpy, whose emotions are reactive and who is still linked to the cultural affairs of this world, cannot develop Samadhi. It is as simple as that. In fact such a person cannot go beyond attempts at dharana, which is effortful linkage of the attention to a higher concentration force, object or person. This is because the mento-emotional energy will remain unstable, locking and unlocking unto various ideas and images which emerge from the memory, come in through sensual perception or are developed by the dull darkish non-glowing buddhi organ.

Until the mento-emotional energy is established by a complete pratyahara sensual withdrawal procedure, the attention will not be freed to focus on the void which occurs before a split second interval between locking and unlocking of the mento-emotional energy. All these factors must be properly mastered before one can get to the dhyana effortless linkage of the attention to higher concentration force, object or person. And when that is mastered by regular practice, then one can do Samadhi which is the contentious effortless linkage of the same.

# Verse 36

sattva-purushayor atyantasankirnayoh pratyayavishesho bhogah
pararthat svarthasanyamat purusha-jnanam

sattva – intelligence energy of material nature; purusayah- of the individual spirit; atyanta- excessively, extremely, very; asamkirnayoh – of what is distinct or separate; pratyayah – mental content, awareness within the psyche; avisesah – not distinct, inability to distinguish; bhogah – experience; pararthatvat – what is apart from another thing; svartha – one own, self interest; samyamat - from the complete restraint of the mentoemotional energy; purusa – individual spirit; jnanam – knowledge

*Experience results from the inability to distinguish between the individual spirit and the intelligence energy of material nature, even though they are very distinct. By complete restraint of the mento-emotional energy while focusing on self-interest distinct from the other interest, a yogi gets knowledge of the individual spirit.*

## Commentary:

To understand this verse we must go back to chapter 2 verses 20 – 25 as follows:

### Verse 20

The perceiver is the pure extent of his consciousness but his conviction is patterned

by what is perceived.

### Verse 21

The individual spirit who is involved in what is seen exists here for that purpose

only.

### Verse 22

It is not effective for one to whom its purpose is fulfilled but it has a common effect

on the others.

### Verse 23

There is a reason for the conjunction of the individual self and his psychological energies. It is for obtaining the experience of his own form.

**Verse 24**

The cause of the conjunction is spiritual ignorance.

**Verse 25**

The elimination of the conjunction which results from the elimination of that spiritual ignorance is the withdrawal that is the total separation of the perceiver from the mundane psychology.

This verse which defines experiences, as being the inability to distinguish between the individual spirit and the intelligent energy of material nature, is the heart of the matter of self realization. It causes us to bow down very low to the Maharishi Mahayogi Sri Patanjali. In a very rare and precise declaration, he out rightly condemns our experiences (bhogas) in material nature.

They come to us because of our ability to distinguish between our spirits and the intelligent energy of material nature. This otherwise called spiritual ignorance or avidya. The implication is this: If we could distinguish between our spirits and the intelligence energy of material nature, then we would not have to take the course of experience (bhogah) through material nature, through the various species of life, in and out of the various subtle and gross dimensions, which are produced in and are formed of subtle and gross material nature. However, there is a way out, which is the focusing on the spirit itself apart from the other interests, which is material nature. Sri Patanjali earmarked, not just material nature but its sattva features or its highest most sensitive and intelligent energy.

This verse 36 is perhaps the most dangerous verse in these sutras. At this point serious students of yoga can close the book and think over what happened. Since they met Patanjali in the form of these sutras, which are his words echoing down the centuries to reach us. It is as if he introduced himself with a very promising statement about giving an explanation of yoga. But then after leading the students down a dark tunnel in which there appeared to be a light, in the distance they found themselves in a dead-ended room with Sri Patanjali pointing a gun at their heads, drawing the trigger dispassionately and letting a bullet in their brains at point blank range.

Sri Patanjali, it appears wants to take away the very life of the living entities, theirexperiences as they know it, since he claims that experiences only occur because we of the inability to distinguish between one's spiritual self and one's psyche or the spiritual self and the psychology on instinctively possessed from material nature. To some students Sri Patanjali recommends a form of death, because they do not know themselves except as that very psychology which they derived from material nature.

# Verse 37

tatah pratibha-shravana-vedanadarshasvada-vartta jayante

**tatah- thence, therefore, from that focus; pratibha- the shining organ of divination; sravana- hearing; vedana- touching; adarsa- sight; asvada-taste; vartah- smell; jayante-is produced**

*From that focus is produced smelling, tasting, seeing, touching and hearing, through the shining organ of divination.*

## Commentary:

Now all of a sudden, after putting the student through the horror, Sri Patanjali continues with some promising statement about yoga development. The student will have to review sutra 36 of this chapter at a later date. It is vital that he understands the implications of it, which is nirvana or the blowing out of the subtle and gross material existence. From complete restraint of the mental and emotional energy and the focusing on the self interests of the spirit, leaving aside completely the interests of material nature, the yogi becomes occupied applying his organ of divination, his developes brahmarandra to all his sensual pursuits. Then, instead of senseing through the mento-emotional energy (citta), he senses directly through by spiritual energy. This was recommended before:

drastr-drsyayoh samyogo heya-hetuh The cause which is to be avoided is the indiscriminate association of the observer and what is perceived. (Yoga Sutra 2.17) The idea that the individual spirit will merge into the absolute and will then be without senses is not given in Patanjali's sutras, even through many yogis and yogi philosophers seem to think so.

# Verse 38

te samadhav upasarga vkyutthane siddhayah

te- they, those abilities; samadhau- in Samadhi continues effortless linkage of the attention to a higher concentration force, object or person; upa sargah- impediments; vyutthane- in expressing, going outwards, rising up; siddhayah- mystic perfectional skills

*Those divination skills are obstacles in the practice of continuous effortless linkage of the attention to a higher concentration force, object or person. But in expressing, they are considered as mystic perfect ional skills.*

## Commentary:

A yogi is stalled if he is distracted for exhibitions of the perfect ional skills which are manifested as he progresses. Those student yogis who cannot resist such exhibitions are doomed. They become premature gurus of a very gullible and stupid public.

# Verse 39

bandha-karana-shaithilyat prachara-sanvedanach cha chittasya
parashariraveshah

bandha- bondage; karana- cause; saithilayat – due to relaxation, collapse;
pracara- channel flow; samvedanat – from knowing; ca – and; cittasya –
of the mento-emotional energies; para – another; sarira – body; avesah
– entrance, penetration

*The entrances into another body is possible by slackening the cause of
bondage and by knowing the channels of the mento-emotional energy.*

### Commentary:

The slackening of the cause of bondage is done by a yogi, when he reaches
the causal level mentioned in verse 35. From the causal place, he is able to
slacken the cause of his having to take his current body. Then he leaves that
body temporarily while it stays in hibernation in Samadhi. He enters forms of
others. A spiritual master may do this after his body dies. He enters into the
forms of his disciples on earth and speaks to small or large audiences, giving
instructions. This prevents him from having to take a new material form. In
that way he remains in the astral world for many years, avoiding physical
rebirth.

Some great yogis like Sri Adi Shankaracarya and Mahayogin Sri Matsyendrana
entered the bodies of others, while their disciples maintain their gross body.
They did this for special purposes. Over all, a student yogi should not endeavor
for this parasariravesah siddhi since it is very dangerous. It is said that recently
in our era, T. Lobsang Rampa who was a Tibetan mystic yogi in his past life,
entered into an Englishman's body after the said occupant agreed to give over
his body in exchange for some merits of Lobsang. Generally such a course is
not recommended for a student yogin.

If one gets in the causal plane and stays there long enough one may develop
an ability to adjust one's resultant reactions which are left in a particular
dimension and which would forestall one's liberation. Thus one may do so
and not have to exhibit the parasarairvesah siddhi. It is not recommended.

If one enters the form of another, one has to go through the channels of his
mento-emotional energy. That entails adopting part of his nature and assuming
some of his responsibilities. That is dangerous since one may forget oneself,
and begin to feel as if one is the other person, all because of becoming too
familiar in identity to that person's psyche. Sri Matyendranath even though
he was a siddha at the time, was rescued by his most advanced disciple, the
mahayogin Sri Goraksnatha. Matsyendranatha entered the body of another
person and forgot his identity after adopting the strangers psyche. In the case
of Sri Adi Shankaracarya, he did not forget himself, but the queen of the King's

body she wanted him to stay on as her husband and not to return to his body. There are dangers in adopting the body of another. It is interesting that a great yogin as Sri Adi Shankara had to enter the almost dead body of a king, just to experience sexual intercourse with a female, because after all a yogi can get such experiences on the astral planes which are near to this world or he may enter a parallel world and get such experiences. It is not necessary to enter any other person's physical body to get such experiences. We must conclude therefore that destiny plays hard cards against a certain yogin at specific stages of his advancement, in order to force him to do certain dangerous and risky things.

Sri Adi Shankaracharya is rated as an incarnation of Lord Siva. From what I learned in the association of the siddhas in the higher astral world, he is Skanda Kumara, the celibate son of Lord Shiva. They claimed that due to his insubordination to Devi, Lord Shiva's wife, he had that difficulty in that incarnation. If one plans to be celibate, one should not expect much help from Goddess Durga, but all the same, She is in a position to cause disruptions in one's yoga practice.

# Verse 40

udana-jayaj jala-panka-kantakadishvasanga utkrantisth cha

udana – air which rises from the throat and enters the head; jayat – from the conquest of; jala – water; panka – mud; kantaka – thorns; adisi – and similar aspects; asangah – non contact; utkrantih – rising above; ca – and

*By mastery over the air which rises from the throat into the head, a yogi can rise over or not have a contact with water, mud or sharp objects.*

## Commentary:

Udana vayu is the air which moves up from the throat area to the top of the head. Initially a yogi controls that in kundalini yoga practice, when he is able to force the apana air, the lowest most polluted air in the body, up and out of the body through the spinal column. Sometimes for connivance sake, one is able to cross water or mud or sharp objects, miraculously even though one may not willfully exhibit such perfect ional power, which was demonstrated by many great yogis before and by Lord Jesus Christ. Certain animals have the natural power since the spirit uses forms which are able to suppressed and regulate the udana vayu. Of course, a yogi's exhibition of that siddhi is something different. The expression of miracles, even though it helps a yogi on the occasion and cause impediments under other conditions. These exhibitions are not recommended. Sri Patanjali lists these to not encourage their use but to alert student yogis of what will happen as they advance through the practice.

# Verse 41

## samana-jayaj jvalanam

**samana- digestive energy ; jayat- conquest ; jvalanam- shining , burning, blazing, with firey glow**

*By conquest of the samana digestive force, a yogi's psyche blazes or shines with a fiery glow.*

### Commentary:

Conquest of the samana digestive force comes by the practice of kundalini yoga which entails various asanas combined with pranayama, especially bhastrika pranayama. By that a yogi gets control over diet. He purifies the navel region of the body. This sets the stage for purification of the sexual functions which opens a gate for the yogi to attack the muladhar anal region. After this is achieved in the downward course, it must be archived in the upward course, as the prana is pushed down and forces the apana energy to move upwards through a subtle tubing called the sushumana nadi. When a yogi on the upward purification course, purifies his navel region, he experiences frontal kundalini. It is then that he achieves conquest over the samana digestive fire. His subtle body then appears with an orangish fiery glow.

# Verse 42

**shrotrakashayoh sanbandha-sanyamad divyam shrotram**

srotra-hearing sense; akasayoh – of space; sambandha- relationship; samyamat- from the complete restraint of the mento-emotional energy; divyam- divine, supernatural; srotram- hearing sense

*By the complete restraint of the mento-emotional energy, while focusing on the hearing sense and space, a yogin develops supernatural and divine hearing.*

## Commentary:

Each yogi masters a particular mystic skill, all depending on the force of practice, on association while progressing and because of his cultural background from many previous lives. By this, particular skills attract his attention. However, if he has the superior association of Lord Shiva, and other mahayogis, he will not invest time in using the mystic skills but will stay focused on the objective of psyche purification; something from which he could quickly gain spiritual perfection.

# Verse 43

kayakashayoh sanbandha-sanyamat laghu-tula-samapattesth
chakashagamanam

kaya – body; akasayoh- of the sky, atmosphere; samyamat- from
the complete restraint of the mento-emotional energy; laghu – light;
tula- cotton fluff; samapatteh – of meeting, of linking; ca- and; akasa-
atmosphere; gamanam- going through, passing through

*By the complete restraint of the mento-emotional energy, which, linking
the mind to the relationship between the body and the sky and linking the
attention to being as light as a cotton fluff, a yogi acquires the ability to
pass through the atmosphere.*

## Commentary:

This does not necessarily mean levitation of the physical body. It can mean
that the use of the subtle body. Since every user of a physical body, already
has a subtle form which can pass through the atmosphere with ease, it is not
necessary to focus on making the physical body as buoyant as a cotton fluff
which can float easily in the air, as if too deny the power of gravity. In addition,
a yogi who can see or hear from afar, would not require that his gross body be
moved from one place to another merely to perceive through it, what he can
divine from a distance.

# Verse 44

bahir akalpita vrittir maha-videha tatah prakashavarana-kshayah

bahir- outside, external; akalpita- not manufactured, not artificial, not formed; vrittih- operation; maha- great; videha – bodiless state; tatah- thence, from that, resulting from that; prakasa- light; avarana – covering, mental darkens; ksayah – dissipation, removal

*By the complete restraint of the mento-emotional energy which is external, which is not formed, a yogi achieves the great bodiless state. From that the great mental darkness which veils the light is dissipated.*

### Commentary:

The great bodiless state, mahavideha, is a special accomplishment of great yogis, who go beyond the causal plane but who do not get an exception to leave this solar system. Because they fail to obtain the exemption for whatever reason, they remain in the unformed, untapped pure mental energy which was not parceled out to individual spirits. They remain free of involvements. Such yogins hardly interact in the cultural world which is so important to a human being. For those great yogis the mental darkness which human beings consistently experience, do not exist. They moved beyond the subtle negative influences of material nature.

# Verse 45

sthula-svarupa-sukshmanvayarthavattva-sanyamad bhuta-jayah

stula- gross form; svarupa – real nature; suksma –subtle; anvaya – following, connection, distribution; arthavatava – purpose, value; samyamat – from the complete restraint of the mento-emotional energy; bhuta – states of matter; jayah – conquest

*By the complete restraint of the mento-emotional energy, while linking the attention to the gross forms, real nature, subtle distribution and value of states of matter, a yogi gets conquest over them.*

## Commentary:

Some yogins are diverted from their progression by too much research into the material nature. However, for them that diversity is necessary, until they reach a stage of more resistance to the material energy. The main asset of a yogi is to keep in touch with more advanced yogins so that even if the student yogin becomes fascinated or stalled somewhere in the practice, his advanced teachers can guide him away from degradation.

# Verse 46

tato 'nimadi-pradurbhavah kaya-sanpat tad-dharmanabhighatash cha

tatah – thence, from that; anandi = anima- minuteness +adi- and the related mystic skills pradurbhavah – coming into existence, manifesting; kaya – subtle body; sampat – wealth, prosperity, perfection; tad – tat= of that; dharma – attributes, functions; anabhighatah- non–obstruction; ca- and

*From minuteness and other related mystic skills come the perfection of the subtle body and the non-obstructions of its functions.*

## Commentary:

When the yogi develops the mystic skills, he finds that the subtle body is perfected to such a degree that the nadis, subtle tubes within it carry a subtle fluid which is as crystal clear as pure water. From certain dimensions this appears to be liquid light traveling through the subtle body of the yogi. Some of this purity filters into the gross body and the yogi is said to perform miracles.

The obstructions a common man experiences, and those a neophyte yogi are fascinated with, are removed from the perfected yogin, because his subtle form is completely purified. The way of operation of the subtle body is obstructed by impurities which arise by attachments to the material energy. When a yogi completes this pratyahar, fifth stage of yoga and when he ceases interactions with the citta mento-emotional energy, thus resting his buddhi organ from involvements and calculation regarding cultural activities, then he reaches the required purity.

# Verse 47

rupa-lavanya-bala-vajra-sanhananatvani kaya-sanpat

rupa – beautiful form; lavanya – charm; bala – mystic force; vajra - diamond-like, infallible; samhananatvani – definiteness, hardness; kaya – subtle body; sampat – perfection

*Beautiful form, charm, mystic force, diamond-like definition come from the perfection of the subtle body.*

## Commentary:

Most commentators give kaya as the physical body. However, in advanced yoga practice, kaya is the subtle body, the temporary but long lasting body which the yogin must perfect before he can attain liberation.

When the subtle body is upgraded by the practice of kundalini yoga, it attains beauty of form, mystic force and diamond-like definition. It attains clarity in it. Its colors become free from cloudiness and vague. It moves into the higher pranic force. It is experienced as a sattva guna body, a form of the mode of pure goodness.

# Verse 48

grahana-svarupasmitanvayarthavattva-sanyamad indriya-jayah

grahana – sensual grasping; svarupa – own form; asmita –identification; anvaya – connection, association; arthavatva – value, worth; samyamat – from the continuous effortless linkage of the attention; indriyajayah- the mastery of the sensual energy by psychological control

*From the continuous effortless linkage of the attention to sensual grasping, to the form of the sensual energy, to its identifying powers, to its connection instinct and to its actual worth, a yogi acquires conquest over his relationship with it.*

## Commentary:

It is important to understand and to accept for oneself, that these achievements occur after prolonged practice. Those who feel they can achieve these overnight will definitely be frustrated. Yoga practice matures and remains firm only after long practice, and not just for one life but through a succession of lives, until the practice becomes an instinct. A yogin must study his own sensual energy. He must also take hints from the way others use their sensual powers. It takes time to accomplish this. The sensual energy is subtle and moves at a rapid rate to execute its functions. It is mostly involuntary, which means that it operates on its own. This makes it difficult to track. However, after long practice, a yogin gets a foothold in these achievement described by Sri Patanjali. One must study how the sensual energy appropriates or grasps subtle phenomena. This is indicated by the term anvaya. One must study how the energy connects with and associates with various types of subtle and gross objects. One must know the form of the sensual energy, its swarupa. This is its form when it does not assume the identity of other objects. One should understand its nature for identification as well as its worth to the self. When all this is achieved, then the yogi gains mastery over his relationship to that sensual force.

# Verse 49

tato manojavitam vikarana-bhavah pradhana-jayash cha

tatah- subsequently; manojavitwam = manah –mind + javitwam – swiftness, rapidity; vikaranabhavah = parting away from, dispersing + karana-creating, making + bhavah- mentoemotional energy, feeling; pradhanah – subtle matter; jayah – conquest; ca – and

*Subsequently, there is conquest over the influence of subtle matter and over the parting away or dispersion of the mento-emotional energy, with the required swiftness of mind.*

## Commentary:

These aspects are on the mystic place. This is attained after long practice at dharana. At first a yogi practices dharana, feeling that he mastered the pratyahar sensual restraint. Thereafter he discovers that he only mastered particular phases of such restraint. Under direction of higher yogis, he goes back to his restraint practice. Then he again returns to dharana. This occurs frequently, until at last his perception of the subtle realities develop fully. What was subtle becomes gross; what was gross fades away completely. He purifies himself even further and grasps more higher reality which used to affect him in lower stages.

# Verse 50

sattva-purushanyata-khyati-matrasya sarvabhavadhishthatritvam
sarvajnatritvam cha

sattva – clarifying perception of material nature; purusa – the spiritual personality; anyata – other than distinct from; khyatimatrasya = khyati – the discriminating faculty of the intellect + matrasya – only; sarva – all; bhava – states of feelings and perceptions; adhisthatratvam – authority, complete disaffection; sarvajnatritvam = sarva –all + jnatritvam – knowledge, intuition; ca – and

*Only when there is distinct discrimination between the clarifying perception of material nature and the spiritual personality, does the yogi attain complete disaffection and all applicative intuition.*

## Commentary:

Khyati means the well-develop truth yielding discrimination of the buddhi organ. But this is attained after long practice only. When this is developed, then the yogi sees clearly at all times the distinction between his spiritual person and the clarifying influences of material nature, influencing from which he took assistance all along.

In advanced yoga, or kriya yoga, one has to maintain the distinction between oneself and the perceiving instruments of the subtle body, even through initially one must take help from those truth yielding perceptions. Adhisthatrtvam means complete or full disaffection from the subtle influence of material nature, even from the clarifying powers which are so helpful.

# Verse 51

## tad-vairagyad api dosha-bija-kshaye kaivalyam

**tadvairagyat = tad (tat) – that + vairagyat – from a lack of interest; api – also, even; dosabijaksaye = dosa - fault, defect + bija- seed, origin, source + ksaye – on elimination; kaivalyam - the absolute isolation of the self from what is lower than itself, isolation of the self from the lower psyche of itself**

## Commentary:

Kaivalyam, which is a popular word in yoga and meditation circles, is greatly mistranslated and misinterpreted. Its meaning is not that the yogi would become one with God. For Patanjali, the master of yoga, never says that in these verses. Kaivalya is the isolation of the self from its lower psyche, such that the subtle mundane instruments of the psyche are separated from the self or atma. The atma becomes freed from it's reliance to those useful domineering subtle tools. Previously Sri Patanjali described Kailvayam in this way: "The elimination of the conjunction which results from the elimination of that spiritual ignorance is the withdrawal that is the total separation of the perceiver from the mundane psychology." It is amazing how so many translators, following the one-ness craze completly distorted Sri

Patanjali by giving so many misleading and totally out-of-context meanings for the term kaivalyam. Vaman Shivram Apte in his practical Sanskrit-English dictionary gives the following plain means for these terms; perfect isolation, soleness, exclusiveness, individuality, detachment of the soul from matter, identification with the Supreme Spirit, final emancipation or beatitude.

As it is with all words, we must seek out the meaning of an author by his definitions and usage. Vaman Shivram Apte hinted at the root of the word from which kaivalyam is derived. He gives this in parenthesis:

*"deva kevalasya bhavah syan"*

He gives Kevalah as peculiar, alone, sole, isolated, whole perfect, absolute, pure simply.

# Verse 52

sthany-upanimantrane sangha-smayakaranam punar anishtaprasangat

sthani – person from the place a yogi would then attain if his material body died; upanimantrane – on being invited; sanga – association; smaya – fascination, wonderment; akaranam - non-responsiveness; punah – again; anista – unwanted features of existence; prasangat – due to association, due to endearing friendliness

*On being invited by a person from the place one would attain if his body died, a yogi should be non-responsive, not desiring their association and not being fascinated, otherwise that would cause unwanted features of existence to arise again.*

## Commentary:

A perfect example of a person who implemented this advice of Sri Patanjali, long before Patanjali took his material body to write the yoga sutras, is Mugala, who in the Mahabharata rejected proposals for transference to the Swarga angelic world. Mugal had reached a stage of progression where he was eligible to live in a special palace of the lord of the angelic world. He was visited by Matali the lord's charioteer, but when questioned by Mudgala, Matali admitted that there were defects in the angelic world, even for great yogins who would go there. They would again (punah) have to revert back to this world after sometime of enjoying paradisiacal enjoyments. Thus Mudgal said that he did not want to go to such a place but would continue his austerities to go somewhere which was devoid of all unwanted features of existence (anista). For others, who are not as strong and determined as Mudgala, it is easier said than done. They may not avoid the temptation of the angelic world. By developing endearing friendless (prasangat), they will succumb to angelic association and the fascinations of such a world. Just as governments of the developed countries skim off the intelligent people from the lesserdeveloped lands, so the angelic people attract the higher minds of the early planets.

# Verse 53

kshana-tat-kramayoh sanyamad vivekajam jnanam

ksana – moment; tat- that; kromayoh – on the sequence; samamat- due to the continuous effortless linkage of the attention; vivekajam – the distinction caused by subtle discrimination; jnanam - knowledge

*By the continuous effortless linkage of the attention to the moment and to the sequence of the moments, the yogi has knowledge caused by the subtle discrimination.*

## Commentary:

Every word in these text must be understood within the content of Patanjali and not just for our own fancy according to our stage of development, agenda of or spiritual mission. To understand Patanjali and to get the most benefit from his sutras, we have to stay with his meanings only, and then try to see where we have progressed to and where we should advance onwards. When a yogi can observe subtle mystic moments and see how they flow on one to another, he develops a very subtle insight which gives definite knowledge of things. Viveka means every subtle insight and jam means what is caused or produced from the super-knowledge of that yogi.

# Verse 54

jati-lakshana-deshair anyatanavachchedat tulyayos tatah pratipattih

jati – type genius, genus, general category; laksana – individual characteristics; desaih – bywhat location; anyata – otherwise, in a different manner; anavacchedat- due to or resulting fromlack of definition; tulyayoh – of two similar types; tatah – hence, subsequently; patipattih –perception

*Subsequently, the yogi has perception of two similar realties which otherwise could notbe sorted due to a lack of definition in terms of their general category, individualcharacteristic and location.*

### Commentary:

Persistence in higher yoga brings on more definition. Things which before, seemed to be on or seem to be merged, appear clearly by their category, individual characteristics and locations. This begins by his sorting out his buddhi intellect organ, its various parts, as well as the sense of identity. A yogi thus develops mystic clarity.

# Verse 55

tarakam sarva-vishayam sarvatha-vishayam akramam cheti vivekajam
jnanam

tarakam - crossing over transcending; sarva – all; visayam - subtle and gross mundane objects; sarvatha – in all ways; visayam – subtle and gross mundane object; akramam – without sequential perceptions; ca- and; iti- thus, subsequently; vivekajam- the distinction caused by subtle discrimination; jnanaam – knowledge

*The distinction caused by subtle discrimination is the crossing over or transcending of all subtle and gross mundane objects in all ways they are presented, without the yogi taking recourse to any other sequential perceptions of mind reliance.*

## Commentary:

Sri Patanjali highlights the culmination of yoga, so that as a yogi we can gage ourselves to know where we are on the course of crossing over the mundane reality which keeps us so occupied when we try to transcend it.

# Verse 56

sattva-purushayoh shuddhi-samye kaivalyam

sattva – intelligence energy of material nature; purusaya- of the spirit; suddhi- purity;samye- on being equal; kaivalyam – total separation from the mundane psychology

*When there is equal purity between the intelligence energy of material nature and thespirit, then there is total separation from the mundane psychology.*

## Commentary:

Readers should check the following verses to understand Sri Patanjali's use of the termssattva, purusayoh and kaivalyam (verse 3.36 and verse 2.25). Obviously the key term in thisverse is sattva. What is sattva? It is clear however that for the aspiring yogi, he must use sattvato become self-realized. This being established, all questions as to why he is to depend onnature is irrelevant. It is not why he has to depend, but rather how he can project himself orcause himself to be situated in alliance with the material nature in its primal purity (suddhisamye).What will happen to him thereafter? Is there something higher? Where will he go afterthat? What will be his status? Is there a world to which he will escape if he attains that? Willthat world have the same purified sattva –energy (intelligence energy of material nature)? Isthere any place or world where he could encounter only energy like his spirit (purusah).These are the questions to be considered by the yogin.

# 4
# Kaivalya-pāda
# (Absolute Independence)

The fourth chapter is about the final attainment of kaivalya which is the term in Yoga Darshana for moksha.

# Verse 1

janmaushadhi-mantra-tapah-samadhijah siddhayah

janma – birth, particular species; ausadhi – drugs; mantra – special sound; tapah – physical bodily austerities in Hatha Yoga; Samadhi – continuous effortless linkage of the attention to a higher concentration force, object or person; jah – what is produced from; siddhayah – mystic skills

*The mystic skills are produced through taking birth in particular species, or by taking drugs, or by reciting special sounds , or by physical bodily austerities or by the – continuous effortless linkage of the attention to a higher concentration force, object or person.*

## Commentary:

The mystic XE "mystic" skills are inherent in the subtle body of each creature but the manifestation of these depends on particular circumstances. Taking birth in a particular species either as an animal, angel, or human being, can cause one to express unusual powers. Taking narcotic drugs or stimulants may cause shifts in pranic force in the subtle body. This would activate some paranormal powers. Repeating special sounds or having these recited on one's behalf might affect the pranic arrangement in one's subtle body, resulting in paranormal powers. And of course yoga austerities in Hatha Yoga would definitely cause the development of psychic powers. Samadhi, which is listed last by Sri Patanjali, is definitely yielding of paranormal perceptions.

# Verse 2

### jaty-antara-parinamah prakrity-apurat

jatyantara =jati – category + antara - other, another; parinamah – transformation; prakriti – subtle material nature; apurat – due to filling up or saturation

*The transformation from one category to another is by the saturation of the subtle material nature.*

### Commentary:

Modern authorities like Timothy Leary and Aldus Huxley, preferred the use of drugs for the development of higher perception. But Sri Gorakshanath wanted us to use the Hatha Yoga austerities. Sri Babaji Mahasaya recommended the Samadhi continuous effortless linkage of the attention to a higher concentration force, object or person. However modern spiritual masters from India usually hawk the mantra special sounds as the means of perfection. And some psychics say that a person should be gifted from birth with mystic abilities.

When a living entity develops a higher quality and when that expression becomes saturated in his nature, he is automatically transferred into a higher species of life, either as an elevated human being, an angelic personality or a divine being.

Sri Babaji Mahasaya gave me a notation for verse one:

"Each of the methods for developing or manifesting the mystic skills are listed in order of the particular efforts made by the yogi. The fist is janma or birth opportunity. That is based on efforts in the past lives. Thus in the current life, no effort is required. Some might take the janma or appearance in higher realms like in siddhaloka. There, taking a siddha yoga body, one experiences the result of his previous austerities. Others take an earthly body again and by the force of their past penance, experience mystic skills even in another gross body.

Ausadhi means hers, drugs or chemical means of adjusting the gross and subtle body. This used to be a method in the Vedic period. This is why one might read about the soma plant. This does not require much endeavor, only the acquirement of the particular plant species. By ingesting that plant in its concentrated form, pranic energy in one's subtle body is affected and certain abilities of the subtle body become manifested. This method was used by shamans, the religious leaders of primitive people.

The herbal method is a risky one, since the dosage may be wrong. It might be too high or too low, too concentrated or too diluted. It might kill or disable the body. Mantra special sounds is the general method preferred by most human beings. This operates confidence energy of the person. By he may or may not succeed in experiencing something about the subtle body. This is an easy method requiring only the working of the vocal chords or silent mental sounding. This method remained popular for thousands of years due to human tendency for relying on hope for calling on superior authority for assistance.

Tapah means the Hatha Yoga austerities which purify both the gross and subtle bodies. This includes kundalini yoga for changing bad subtle energy. This is the classic method for attaining purity of the intelligence energy of material nature; an energy mentioned in verse 56 of the last chapter:

When there is equal purity between the intelligence energy of material nature and the spirit, then there is total separation from the mundane psychology.
(Yoga Sutra 3.56)

If that energy is not purified, then the progress will be erratic causing the yogi to fall to a lower level sooner or later. The Hatha Yoga austerities are the definite way for such purity. Study what Krishna said in the chapter 65 verse 12 of His Bhagavd –Gita discourse.

The last method which is the best is Samadhi, the continuous effortless linkage of the attention to a higher reality. This is the choice method. However this is merely an advancement of the tapah or Hatha Yoga austerity method. It does not stand alone. One cannot attain Samadhi without doing the Hatha Yoga austerities proficiently.

In summary, janma means efforts in a past life. Ausadhi means eating, drinking, smelling or otherwise ingesting chemicals which affects the sublet body. Mantra means using ones faith or confident energy. Tapah means physical austerities which eradicate impurities in the subtle form. Samadhi means using ones psychic force to reach higher realities.

# Verse 3

nimittam aprayojakam prakritinam varanabhedas tu tatah kshetrikavat

nimittam – cause, motive, apparent cause ; aprayojakam – not used, not employed, not causing; prakrtinam – of the subtle material energy; varana – impediments, obstacles; bhedah – splitting, removing, disintegrating; tu – but , except; tatah – hence; ksetrikavat – like a farmer

*The motivating force of the subtle material energy is not used except for the disintegration of impediments, hence it is compared to a farmer.*

## Commentary:

Even though a yogin is assisted by material nature, which exhibits powerful motivating forces from time to time, still his spiritual progress is not really caused by nature. It is just that sometimes nature removes its own forces which acted as impediments to the efforts of the yogi.Even though a farmer does so many things to facilitate the growing of seeds, still that does not mean that any of his actions are the real causes of plant growth. The development from seeds to plant has more to do with the potential within the seed that it does with the farmer's efforts. Similarly material nature does not cause a yogi's development, even though nature may facilitate that progression.

# Verse 4

**nirmana-chittany asmita-matrat**

**nirmana** – producing, creating, measuring, fabricating; **cittani** – regions within in the mento-emotional energy; **asmita** – sense of identity which is developed in relation to material nature; **matrat** – from that only

*The formation of regions within the mento-emotional energy, arises only from the sense of identity which is developed in relation to material nature.*

**Commentary:**

Even though the spirit's attention is one only, still because of the mento-emotional energy, there appears to be various regions within the mind and feelings of a personality. A yogi by mystic research in kriya yoga, within his psyche, traces all these mental regions and emotional moods to the sense of identity which he experiences anytime his attention goes in the direction of the gross or subtle material nature. Thus eventually he develops a disgust (virvedah), and becomes very serious about spiritual progression. He no longer wants to be entertained by the various imaginings within the mind.

# Verse 5

pravritti-bhede prayojakam chittam ekam anekesham

pravrtti – frantic activity, disperal of energy; bhede – in the difference; prayojakam – very, much used or employed; cittam – the mento-emotional energy; ekam – one; anekesam – of what is numberless

*The one mento-emotional energy is that which is very much used in numberless different dispersals of energy?*

## Commentary:

With this in mind, a yogi takes steps to stop the innumerable impulsive operations of the mind.

# Verse 6

tatra dhyanajam anashayam

**tatra** – there, in that case; **dhyanajam** – produced by the effortless linkage of the attention to a higher reality; **anasayam** – without harmful emotions

*In that case only subtle activities which are produced from the effortless linkage of the attention to a higher reality are without harmful emotions.*

## Commentary:

Asayam is the seat of feelings, the place in the mento-emotional energy with which is derived endearing but harmful emotions. This location is difficult to tract since it is in a mystic domain. Until a yogi gets clarity of consciousness he cannot transcend his feelings.He is continually fooled by them. When he masters the effortless linkage of the mind to higher realities, then he gains objectively and can sort out the endearing but harmful feelings, even the memory which is a storehouse of these.

# Verse 7

**karmashuklakrishnam yoginas trividham itaresham**

**karma – cultural activity; asukla – not white, not rewarding; akrsnam – not black, not penalizing; yoginal – of the yogis; trividham – three-fold; irtaresam - for others**

*The cultural activity of the yogis is neither rewarding nor penalizing, but others have three types of such action.*

## Commentary:

An advanced yogi who has mastered the dhyana effortless linkage of the mind to a higher reality, may perform cultural activities, just as others do but for him, these do not result in rewarding, penalizing nor fruitless results.

What then does the yogi gain from cultural activities? He gains absolutely nothing, because his detachment allows the reactions to fall back into material nature without a claimant.

# Verse 8

tatas tad-vipakanugunanam evabhivyaktir vasananam

tatah – subsequently; tad – that, those; vipaka – development, fruition; anugunanam – of the corresponding features; eva - only, alone; abhivyaktih – manifestation; vasananam – of tendencies within the mento-emotional energy

*Subsequently from those cultural activities there is development according to corresponding features only, bringing about the manifestation of the tendencies within the mento-emotional energy.*

**Commentary:**

Everything in the material creation works according to innate tendency, manifesting according to time and place. Sometimes it takes thousands of years before something can manifest or be given any type of satisfaction.

In terms of the time of the earth, modern civilization is very recent. Still we see that the majority of people feel comfortable within the modern world. This is due to latent desires, which are being fulfilled under the present circumstances.

Because a yogi has mystic insight, he understands how numberless different dispersals of energy arise in the mento-emotional force by its proximity to the spirits sense of identity. Thus withdraws that sense and de-activates the mundane consciousness, freeing himself from being a slave to desires which arise in the seat of feelings. Others however must comply with the urges.

# Verse 9

jati-desha-kala-vyavahitanam apy anantaryam smriti-
sanskarayorekarupatvat

jati – status; desa – location; kala – time; vyavahitanam – of what is placed apart or separated; api – even, also; anantaryam – timeful sequence; smrti – memory; samskarayoh – of the impressions formed of cultural activities; ekarupatvat – due to one form

*Even though circumstances are separated by status, location and time, still the impressions form cultural activities and the resulting memories, are of one form and operate on a time full sequence.*

## Commentary:

This has to do with why past lives affect the present one, even though the individual may or may not recall his past. A different status, a different place and a different time, though separated from a cultural activity of the past, is in fact time full and in sequence according to how it was laid into the memory within the mento-emotional energy of the individual concerned. Something that makes sense subjectively may seem totally misappropriate to the conscious mind which takes into account only what it can grasp about the present. Irrespective of the present circumstances, the memory and the urges from past lives, operate in timeful sequence.

# Verse 10

tasam anaditvam chashisho nityatvat

tasam – those; anaditvam – what is without beginning, primeval; ca – and; asisah – hope and desire energies; nityatvat – what is eternal

*Those memories and impressions are primeval, without a beginning, hope and desire energies are eternal as well.*

### Commentary:

When a yogi sees that the hope and desire energy is eternal, he makes a decision to let it be and to detach himself from the urges. He must, by all means, get himself separated from the mento-emotional force or remain a victim of it. The memories and the circumstance-forming impressions will be there for all eternity.A yogin has no choice but to extract his existence from the realm of it.

# Verse 11

hetu-phalashrayalambanaih sangrihitatvad esham abhave tad-abhavah

**hetu** – cause; **asraya** – storage place, causal plane supportive base; **alambanaih** – by what supports or lifts; **sangrhitatvat** – what holds together; **esam** – of those, these; **abhave** – in what is not there; **tad** – them; **abhavah** – not existing

*They exist by what holds them together in terms of cause and effect, supportive base and lifting influence. Otherwise if their causes are not there, they have no existence whatsoever.*

### Commentary:

For a yogi, his involvement is the supportive element which makes the subtle material nature exist for him and engage him or use his consciousness. Thus if he detaches himself the supportive element being removed, material nature no longer affects him.

# Verse 12

atitanagatam svarupato 'sty adhva-bhedad dharmanam

atita – the past; anagatam – the future; svaruptah – true form; asti - there is, it exists; adhvabhedat – due to different courses or events; dharmnam – of the characteristics

*There is a true form of the past and future denoted by the different courses of their characteristics.*

## Commentary:

Sri Patanjali establishes that the past and future are real existences, having contents, which cause the present. Time is not an illusion. It is real in that sense. Because of definite characteristics, there is a certain course which time takes from the past into the present and into the yet-emerging future. The inherent characteristics (dharmanam) from the past mold the future. The changes which come about in the present are stockpiled by time as the basis for slight or major differences which are to come.

# Verse 13

te vyakta-sukshmah gunatmanah

**te** – they; **vyakta** – gross; **suksmah** – subtle; **gunatmanah** = guna – subtle material nature + atmanah – of itself

*They are gross or subtle, all depending on their inherent nature.*

**Commentary:**

The three phases of time, the past, present and future, are perpetual, having a relationship one with the other. They are reliant of their inherent energies which comprise the subtle and gross material nature. A limited being cannot permanently affect these, even though he may take part in their operations according to how he is positioned in time and place.

# Verse 14

parinamaikatvad vastu-tattvam

**parinama – transformation, change ; ekatvat – singleness, uniqueness; vastu – object tattvam – essence, actual composition**

*The actual composition of an object is based on the uniqueness of the transformation.*

## Commentary:

Each object no mater how similar, has certain unique qualities which are based on the particular transformations which caused its production. The varieties in material nature are researched by a yogi. Underlying all this, he finds the manifesting force of time along with the inherent qualities of material nature, mixed in various ways.

# Verse 15

vastu-samye chitta-bhedat tayor vibhaktah panthah

vastu – object; samye – in the same; citta – mento-emotional energy; bhedat – from the difference; tayoh – of these two; vibhaktah - separated, divided; panthah - ways of viewing, prejudices

*Because of a difference in the mento-emotional energy of two persons, separate prejudices manifest in their viewing of the very same object.*

## Commentary:

Separate prejudices lie dormant in the mento-emotional energy of each living entity. When viewing the same object which has the same composition, persons react differently. These prejudices are sponsored in material nature by the time which regulates itself in past, present and future.

# Verse 16

**na chaika-chitta-tantram vastu tad-apramanakam tada kim syat**

na – not, nor; a – and; eka – one; citta – mento-emotional perception; tantram – dependent; ced = cet – if, otherwise; vastu – object; tat – that; apramanakam – not being observed; tada – then; kim – what; syat – would occur

*An object is not dependent on one person's mento-emotional perception. Otherwise, what would happen if it were not being perceived by that one person?*

### Commentary:

Sri Patanjali refutes the idea that world is dependent on a limited mind or on a group of such minds. Otherwise if that or those limited minders were to lose perception of any object the item would no longer exist.

# Verse 17

tad-uparagapekshitvach chittasya vastu jnatajnatam

tad =tat- that; uparaga – color, mood; apeksitvat – from the expectation; cittasya – of the mento-emotional energy; vastu – object; jnata –known; ajnatam - unknown

*An object is known or unknown, all depending on the mood and expectation of the particular mento-emotional energy of the person in reference to it.*

## Commentary:

The application or non-application of consciousness is what brings objects into purview.

# Verse 18

sada jnatasth chitta-vrittayas tat-prabhoh purushasyaparinamitvat

sada – always; jnatah- known; citta- mento-emotional energy; vrttayah- the operations; tat- that; prabhoh- of the governor; purusasya – of the spirit; aparinamitvat – due to changelessness

*The operations of the mento-emotional energy are always known to that governing because of the changelessness of that spirit.*

## Commentary:

Here an explanation is given as to why the spirit appears to be affected by the operations of the mento-emotional energy of the psyche. It is due to the changelessness of the spirit, which serves as a background for the movements of consciousness.

# Verse 19

na tat svabhasam drishyatvat

na – not; tat-that; svabhasam- self-illuminative; drsyatvat - for it is due to being something to be perceived

*That mento-emotional energy is not self-illuminative for it is rather only capable of being perceived.*

## Commentary:

The mento-emotional energy has for its nature the capability of being perceived but is not self-illuminative. This has to be studied objectively in meditation by the particular yogin.

# Verse 20

eka-samaye chobhayanavadharanam

ekasamaye – at the same time; ca – and; ubhaya – both; anavadharanam – of what cannot focus

*It cannot execute the focus of both at the same time.*

### Commentary:

This means that the mento-emotional energy cannot both focus on itself and the seer at the same time. This has to be verified in deep meditation.

# Verse 21

chittantara-drishye buddhi-buddher atiprasangah smriti-sanskarah cha

cittantara – drsye = citta – mento-emotional energy + antara- another person + drsye – in the perception of; buddhi-buddher = buddhi- the intellect organ + buddheh – of the intellect organ; atiprasangah – absurd argument, unwarranted stretching of a rule or argument; smrti – memory; sankaras – confusion; ca- and

*In the perception of mento-emotional energy by another such energy, there would be an intellect perceiving another intellect independently. That would cause absurdity and confusion of memory.*

## Commentary:

Sri Patanjali states here that it is absurd to think that without a spirit one mind could perceive another mind. It would be absurd. Unless there is a spirit behind a mind, there would be no perception in that energy.

# Verse 22

chiter apratisankramayas tad-akarapattau svabuddhi-sanvedanam

citeh - of the spirit; apratisamkramayah - not moving from one position to another; tad – tat- that; akara – form, aspect; apattau- turning into, changing, assuming; sva - itself, oneself; buddhi- intellect organ; samvedanam - perception

*The perception of its own intellect occurs when it assumes that form in which there is no movement from one operation to another.*

## Commentary:

Until the mind is still and the mento-emotional energy ceases to fluctuate, one cannot perceive one's intellect objectively. Otherwise, one feels as though oneself and one's intellect were part of an homogeneous consciousness.

# Verse 23

**drashtri-drishyoparaktam chittam sarvartham**

drastr - the perceiver; drsya – the perceived; uparaktam – prejudiced; cittam – mento-emotional energy; sarvartham - what is all evaluating

*The mento-emotional energy which is prejudiced by the perceiver and the perceived is all evaluating.*

## Commentary:

When the mento-emotional force absorbs energy from the spirit, as well as from an object, it seems to be all-evaluating. Thus the spirit becomes absorbed by its operations of analysis, conclusion and action.

# Verse 24

tad asankhyeya-vasanabhish chitram api parartham sanhatya-karitvat

tat – that; asankhyeya – innumerable; vasanabhih – subtle impressions; citram – diversified; api – even, although; parartham – for another's sake; samhatya – because of it

*Although the mento-emotional energy is diverse by innumerable subtle impressions, it acts for the sake of another power because of it's proximity to that other force.*

## Commentary:

Everything done by the mento-emotional energy, even those subtle actions which seem to imperil the spirit are done for the sake of the spirit itself, even though the spirit may not deliberately motivate the psyche.

The proximity (samhatya) of the spirit is itself, the cause of the innumerable moods and urges.

# Verse 25

vishesha-darshina atma-bhava-bhavana-vinivrittih

**visesa – distinction, specific perception; darsina – of the one who sees; atma – the spirit; bhava – feeling; bhavana – absorption in feelings; nivrttih - total stopping of the operations of the mento-emotional energy**

*There is total stopping of the operations of mento-emotional energy for the person who perceives the distinction between feelings and the spirit itself.*

## Commentary:

This is repeated again and again in different verses. A yogin has to sort out between his spirit and his mento-emotional energy. He has to transcend the proximity of the two.

# Verse 26

tada hi viveka-nimnam kaivalya-pragbharam chittam

tada – then; hi – indeed; viveka – discrimination; nimnam – leaning towards, inclined to; kaivalya - total separation from the mundane psychology; prag – towards; bharam – gravitating; cittam – mento-emotional force

*Then, indeed, the mento-emotional force is inclined towards discrimination and gravitates towards the total separation from the mundane psychology.*

## Commentary:

The yogi has to achieve this. It does not come by wishful thinking. Only through higher yoga can this be achieved consistently.

# Verse 27

tach-chidreshu pratyayantarani sanskarebhyah

tat- that; chidresu – in the relaxation of the focus; pratyaya – conviction or belief as mind content, inlaid impression in the mento-emotional energy; antarani – in between, interval; samskarebhah - from the subtle impressions

*Besides that, in the relaxation of the focus, other mind contents arise in the intervals. These are based on subtle impressions.*

## Commentary:

The yogi has to work through this without being disappointed or frustrated. He should not give up the higher yoga practice. He faces failures at every step but he must forge ahead. He must work for emancipation from his helpless alliance with the mento-emotional force. His main energy is the mind's content, which is deeply inlaid, in the mento-emotional force as urg-producing impressions from the past. Some of these surfaces as memory and others surface as pictures, sound formation, and then are expanded into meaningful or meaningless picturizations and sounds which distract the yogi by keeping him occupied in the picture-sound show of the mind. A yogi has to fight this to gain self-conquest.

# Verse 28

hanam esham kleshavad uktam

**hanam – illing off, complete removal; esam – of these; klesavad = klesavat – like the mento-emotional afflictions; uktam – authoritively said**

*As authoritively stated, the complete removal of these is like the elimination of the mento-emotional afflictions.*

### Commentary:

It is a personal struggle. The God is there but each yogi has to master this himself. As a beginning yogi becomes pre-occupied removing all causes for the mental and emotional troubles, so the advanced yogi has to remove the mind content which poses a botheration and which the mind clings to automatically when it relaxed from the proper focus.

Great yogis went on before, but they cannot help us because this is a personal inner struggle. They encourage us to practice. They have shown the way by their personal lives on earth, or by their current austerities in higher dimensions. Besides that, each yogi has to endure this inner conflict alone.

# Verse 29

prasankhyane 'py akusidasya sarvatha viveka-khyater dharma-meghah samadhih

prasamkhyana – in the abstract meditation; api – even so; akusidasya - of one who has no interest or sees no gain in material nature; sarvatha – in all ways; vivekakhyateh - with super discrimination; dharmameghah = dharma - natures way of acting for beneficial results + meghah – mento-emotional clouds of energy; Samadhi- continuous effortless linkage of the attention to higher reality

*For one who sees no gains in material nature, even while perceiving it in abstract meditation, he has the super discrimination. He attained the continuous effortless linkage of the attention to higher reality which is described as knowing the mento-emotional clouds of energy which compel a person to perform according to nature's way of acting for beneficial results.*

### Commentary:

Dharma – meghah is usually translated as cloud (meghah) of virtue (dharma). However we took hints from I. K. Taimni, where he stated that dharma - meghaha- Samadhi, means the final Samadhi in which the yogi shakes himself free from the world of Dharmas which obscure Reality like a cloud.

He is perhaps, the first commentator who understood Sri Patanjali. That is to be regretted. The key to the meaning of this verse lies in the terms akusidasya. This is because kusida means a moneylender, or any money lent at a rate exceeding 5%. When "a" is added as a prefix, it means not having any desire to gain anything.

Srila Yogeshwarananda asked us to develop praravairagya, which is complete disinterest in this world.Sri Patanjali was specific in stating that one has to lose interest even in the very subtle aspect of material nature, aspects which we encounter in deep meditation on other levels of this reality. This is indicated by the term prasamkhyane which means that one may see something of value in deep meditation, in which case one cannot develop the paravairagya and one will not lose interest in the Dharmas or ways of righteous living which are legated by material nature for different beings on different gross and subtle levels.

If we want to benefit in any way (sarvatha) from material nature, on any level, we will be attracted proportionally, and we will fall under the cloud (megha) of values (dharmas) which dictate how we should act to gain in the particular realm of our interest. This will keep us in the material world.

Srila Yogeshwaranada, who warned this writer in the same way, that the main obstacle is the desire for name as a spiritual master, forewarns all yogis. From that comes the idea that one should develop a territory where one can have his own kingdom with loyal disciples. Material nature will then show one a layout of values which one must adapt for success as territorial spiritual master or god. This will cause a fall down. Be forewarned.

Even though Srila Yogeswarananda had left behind many books, as well as ashrams and spiritual missions, still when I see him come down from the causal level where he is completing more austerities and researched into our complication, I never see him with disciples. He is not interested in any of the rules and regulations or dharmas which are laid out for spiritual masters who want to be worshipped as exalted saviors or gurus.

Everything in the material world, in the subtle, super-subtle or gross parts of it, are dangerous. We should know this. There were many people who came to me to be disciples and who suggested that they become elevated so that they can help others. All of them are conceited.

# Verse 30

tatah klesha-karma-nivrittih

**tatah** – subsequently; **klesa** – afflictions; **karma** – cultural activities; **nivrttih** – stoppage of the operation of the mento-emotional energy

*Subsequently there is stoppage of the operation of the mento-emotional energy in terms of generation of cultural activities and their resulting afflictions.*

### Commentary:

The meaning of dharma-meghah in the preceding verse is now explained by the subsequently result of the stoppage of generation of cultural activities which are themselves dictated by various types of dharma righteous life style for particular results in the gross or subtle mundane world. None of these karmas or cultural activities are completely free from afflictions. Thus when the yogi reaches the causal level and sees the various clouds of energy (meghah) in which the dharmas or laws for righteous life, are created and maintained, he gets an ease in his higher yoga practice. He smiles for he will never again fall into the trap of making spiritual missions to help or to save others. Such things are a complete farce, and very disgusting to one who has seen the reality as it is.

An example of a yogin who left aside such things is Swami Satyananda of Bihar, who though he complete all duties given to him by his spiritual master, the great Swami Shivananda, did not himself continue to be a guru in this world, but carefully and efficiently left all that aside to proceed honestly with his advancement. Such a high-class person is neither selfish nor conceited. If anything, he is realistic.

# Verse 31

tada sarvavarana-malapetasya jnanasyanantyaj jneyam alpam

tada – then; sarva – all; avarana - mental darkness; mala – impurities; apetasya - of what is removed; jnanasaya - of knowledge; anantyat – due to being unlimited; jneyam – what is known; alpam- small trivial

*Then, because of the removal of all mental darkness and psychological impurities, that which can be known through the mento-emotional energy, seems trivial in comparison to the unlimited knowledge available when separated from it.*

## Commentary:

For this world, the mento-emotion energy is the linking agent. It is the means of praying into various things. It shows us how to be interested in and how to invest in this world for a benefit. But once we become freed from that energy, and we experience the self by itself, we no longer consider this world as being essential.

# Verse 32

tatah kritarthanam parinama-krama-samaptir gunanam

tatah – thus; krtarthanam – having done their purpose; parinama – changes, alteration; karma – a step, succession, progression, process of development; samaptir = samaptih – end conclusions; gunanam – of the influence of the subtle material nature

*Thus, the subtle material nature, having fulfilled its purpose, its progressive alterations end.*

## Commentary:

This is only for the yogin who achieved isolation from his mento-emotional energies and their impulsive operations.For him, the natural power transfer from his spirit to the mento-emotional force ceases. For others it continues just as before.

# Verse 33

kshana-pratiyogi parinamaparanta-nirgrahyah kramah

ksana – moment; pratiyogi - corresponding, being a counter-part; parinama - change, alteration; aparanta - the end; nirgrahyah - clearly perceived; kramah - process

*The process, of which moments are a counterpart, and which causes the alterations, comes to an end and is clearly perceived.*

## Commentary:

The advanced yogi alone achieves this. This is an individual accomplishment, where the yogi sees the moments, which in sequence make up time which is itself the changing mundane energy (gunanam). The yogi clearly perceives this from afar. What hypnotizes other and keeps them under its control subjectively and objectively, is looked upon by the yogin, just as the God would normally see it.

*sa esah purvesam api guruh kalena anavacchedat*

He, this particular person, being unconditioned by time is the guru even of the ancient teachers, the authorities from before. (Yoga Sutra 1.26)

What is natural for god, becomes natural for the yogin who made that much endeavor and who completed the course of higher yogi described by Sri Patanjali Muni.

# Verse 34

purushartha-shunyanam gunanam pratiprasavah kaivalyam svarupa-
pratishtha va chiti-shakter iti

purusartha- the aims of a human being; sunyanam- devoid of; gunanam-
of the influences of material nature; pratiprasavah- re-absorption,
retrogression, neutralization; kaivalyam- separation of the spirit from
psychology; swarupa- own form; pratistha- established; va- thus, at last

*Separation of the spirit from the mento-emotional energy (kaivalyam)
occurs when there is neutrality in respect to the influence of material
nature, when the yogi's psyche becomes devoid of the general aims of a
human being. Thus at last, the spirit is established in its own form as the
force empowering the mento-emotional energy.*

## Commentary:

This ends the Yoga description of higher yoga practice, given to us by Sri
Patanjali Muni, that authority for all times. Undoubtedly, Sri Patanjali
Mahamuni covered everything in the mystic practice of yoga. All glories unto
him.